KASSULKE

KASSULKE

●

BY
Karl Kassulke
and
Ron Pitkin

THOMAS NELSON PUBLISHERS
Nashville

Published in Nashville, Tennessee, by Thomas Nelson, Inc., Publishers and
distributed in Canada by Lawson Falle, Ltd., Cambridge, Ontario.

Printed in the United States of America.

Scripture texts used in Chapter 34 are taken from the NEW AMERICAN
BIBLE, copyright © 1970, by the Confraternity of Christian Doctrine,
Washington, D. C., and are used by permission of copyright owner. All rights
reserved.

Library of Congress Cataloging in Publication Data:

Kassulke, Karl.
  Kassulke

  1. Kassulke, Karl.   2. Christian biography—United States.   3. Football players—United States—Biography.   I. Pitkin, Ronald E.,
1942–   . II. Title.
BR1725.K34A35   796.332′092′4 [B]   81–11168
ISBN 0-8407-4090-5   AACR2

To Jesus Christ, who is my Lord and Savior,
and John, who introduced me to Him;

and to Susan, Kurt, Kory, and Christopher,
by whom my life has been so richly blessed.

CONTENTS

●

Foreword

Let me introduce you to a good friend.

Karl Kassulke is one of those people nobody ever forgets. There is a quality about him that brings out the best in people, and his generosity is legendary. Whether it was on the practice field or in the locker room, in the crucial moment of a key game or in the quiet moment of shared friendship, in the clowning around of the practical joke or in the serious business of raising money for crippled children—Karl was always there. He was always sparkling with joy. And he always made things better for having been there.

He's still that kind of person. Most people who suffer a severe tragedy like Karl experienced are tempted to quit. But a severed spine and severe brain damage have hardly slowed him down. He's overcome it all, and his story is a testimony to how strong the human spirit can be, especially when it is surrounded by love.

In the final analysis, that's what this story is all about—love. Karl is one of those people who have an extra capacity for it—both in giving and receiving—and that is what makes him so unforgettable. Everyone who comes to know him notices this, and you will, too.

So, welcome to this book. In it you will meet a man who is loved and respected by the people who played with and against him on the football field, as well as those who have known him off it. But Karl was more than just another football player. He was "Hunkie"—the effervescent practical joker, the guy you could count on for help, an ambassador of goodwill to all, a giver and winner, a friend, a Viking.

Yes, this is a book for football fans. The stories are certainly here. But it is also a book for people in love with life. And if you love life, then you'll love *Kassulke*.

—Fran Tarkenton

KASSULKE

CHAPTER 1

So Good
To Run Again

●

The pain.

Oh yeah, the pain.

Why doesn't it stop? My chest. . . . My heart feels like it's pounding out of it! And my breath. I can hardly breathe. Oh, God, what's happening?

It's black in here. I can't see a thing. Feels like I'm in a cave. Trapped in a cold, sweaty, stinking cave. Am I dead? Wouldn't surprise me.

What a sickening feeling.

Feeling? That's a joke—I can't feel anything. Only that pounding, driving pain in my chest and back.

Man, I really can't feel anything. Where are my feet? My legs? What's happened to them? Wait a minute. . . . I can feel my hands. Yeah, I can really feel them. And my head, too.

Oh, where am I?

"Willard! Mom! . . . . Susan! Help! . . . . Dad, help me! Somebody! Somebody help me! I can't move! I can't feel! I can't. . . ."

Snap! Light. I'm in a large bedroom.

I recognize it now. It's mine. I'm home. And Susan is half lying down, half leaning over me.

"Karl! It's alright. It's me, Sue. It's me. Everything's OK. You're just having another dream. You'll be OK."

"Huh? Wha. . . . Oh! Oh, Susan. We were kicking the Packers' tails and taking numbers. It was just like old times. I even blocked that Mike Mercer field goal again."

She's smiling at me now, and the fear is gone from her eyes. "Yes, Karl. That one has been blocked more than any other in the history of the NFL, hasn't it!"

13

"Do you think so? I bet you're right. Haw! If poor old Mike only knew!"

She's laughing now.

"Sue, it was just like that game in Milwaukee . . . just a few blocks from where I grew up. I was running. Really. I really was. It felt so good to run again. And I sacked Bart Starr all over again. And then I stuffed that rookie and blocked the kick . . . right here . . . in my chest. It was . . . it was just like old times, I tell ya. The pain felt so good. And then I woke up. . . . And then I was so scared."

"So was I, Karl. But it's awful late. Let's get back to sleep. You're OK now.

"Good night, Karl."

"Good night."

What a joy! Susan loves me just the way I am. It's too good to be true. What a delight to have her near. How blessed I am. A lot of good, happy memories. Two strong sons. A loving wife. And a baby on the way.

Oh, God, thank you! Thank you.

CHAPTER 2

Easy Rider

●

July 24, 1973.

It was one of those beautiful summer days, the kind that entices so many people to vacation in Minnesota. The sky was clear, the sun bright and hot.

"It's got to be eighty degrees out here today!" I yelled into the wind.

Monty Krizan and I were cruising along the interstate on the Honda 750 I had acquired shortly after Jan asked me to move out of the house. Monty worked with me at the Left Guard restaurant in Bloomington. I was the sports celebrity there, and he was the bartender. Because we both liked to live fast and dangerously, we had become friends quickly.

"More like eighty-five or ninety," Monty laughed. "A great day for hitting the beaches, right? Want to look at the merchandise before you buy it?"

Now I'm laughing.

It had been a rough year and a half. I'd always thought a person worked things out in a marriage. No matter how tough it got, people shouldn't quit. But Jan and I had.

God knows I tried. We went to counselors, argued, fought—all to no avail. In the end she was insistent, and that was that.

It hurt me bad, though, and it still hurt. But I chose to drown my sorrows, not bothering to ask the real questions. Just running. And racing. And chasing. No grass under these wheels!

And I kept laughing.

As the wind battered my face, I remembered the joking Monty and I had enjoyed that morning. We had just finished a five-mile run, our concession to Monty's guilt over raising hell and drinking at all hours with somebody who in a few short days would have to put his body on the line at the Minnesota Vikings' training camp. Training camp was no five-mile run. It wouldn't make much difference how good my condition was when I entered camp, since the coaches would make life miserable regardless. But I didn't have the heart to tell Monty that. So we ran.

We'd been laughing about how we couldn't believe that people actually lived the way we were living. I was telling him how we really ought to do our girl-watching at the beaches.

"You can see what you're getting so much better that way, Monty."

At least it would be better than what was happening around the bars.

"Dirty old man!" That's what he called me. It made for a good laugh. We were full of them.

Before we could hit the beaches, though, we had to go see my accountant, Lowell Gordon, at his office out west on Highway 55. Lowell was going to tell us how we could work out an agreement so that Monty could manage my bar in Mankato and become a working partner. He was convinced that if he were running the place, he could make some real money for both of us.

After seeing Lowell we were planning to have a lazy afternoon. Later on we would drive to the Vikings' training camp on the campus of Mankato State College. I was already happy about going down there. Some of my best memories were of good times with the Hacker and all the rest of my friends on the team, and I was ready for more.

Monty was going to keep my bike at his place since Bud Grant, head coach of the Vikings, had made his views very clear. "Absolutely no bikes in training camp. One of you guys could get hurt. And we don't need that." We all knew better than to break that rule.

So, we had gone out to see Lowell, and he had given us some helpful ideas about how we could set up the business. On our way out of the building, some people from the next office saw us and came out to talk. Before we made it outside we were stopped several more times, and just as we got to my Honda someone called me inside again.

"Monty, how'd you like to drive this thing?"

"I'd love to!"

We traded helmets, and I went back inside to shake hands. When I came back outside, Monty had the cycle ready to go. I put on his helmet, and we headed west out Highway 55. Then we turned south on the interstate.

We were cruising at nearly seventy. For three miles we laughed and joked about those girls on the beach who were just going to have to miss us today, and then the bike began to spit and cough. Monty pulled off the road onto the grass shoulder.

"Karl, will you ever fill this thing before it runs out of gas?"

"Rats! I was going to do it this morning and forgot."

Monty reached down to the valve for the reserve tank. "Well, at least you had the reserve shut off. I think it'll start now. Should be fifteen, maybe twenty miles in 'er yet." Monty started the bike, and again we accelerated to seventy.

We had a clear road ahead of us. There was an eighteen wheeler in our lane, maybe a quarter mile up the road, and another car ahead of it. We began to sing "Buffalo Gals Won't You Come Out Tonight" at the top of our voices. I had picked that one up at a Kiwanis Club meeting in Iowa earlier that year. Monty could sing about as well as I could laugh, so we made much more noise than music.

Monty began to sing another song.

I think we both began to feel the sand and gravel at about the same time. All semis kick up a lot of little stones on hard-surfaced roads, and we were catching up with this one rather fast. We had been enjoying ourselves so much that we hadn't realized that the long hill had slowed the truck to about fifty-five.

The sand began to sting. Sometimes it will even stick in the skin, so I wanted to get out from behind the semi immediately.

"Pass him! Pass him, Monty!"

He'd already signalled. He was checking his mirror just to be sure, and then he laid the bike over to pass the truck. As he did, he gave it a little gas to get around it quickly. Just as we came out from behind the truck, we also broke the crest of the hill.

I was stunned.

There, maybe 100 to 150 feet ahead of us, was a car in the fast lane. Where had it come from? It took me a split second to realize that it was sitting at a dead stop. Why would anyone in their right mind make a U-turn out of the fast lane of the freeway?

I grabbed Monty around the waist.

"Monty, look out! We're going to hit that. . . ."

CHAPTER 3

Road Show

●

We hit the car square, right in the center of the trunk.
We didn't even have enough time to use the brakes.

MONTY KRIZAN:

I can still smell the odor from that trunk. A whole gust
of musty air exploded in my face with a loud "shoosh!"
and to this day I get nauseated whenever I smell an odor
like that.

I've never heard such noise in all my life. Seven years
later I can still hear it clearly. Especially at night. When
we hit the car, the bike buried itself in the trunk, peeling
the bumper and trunk forward and upward. This created
a catapult that threw Karl free and clear of the car.

I was thrown from the bike, too, but the handles and
the trunk absorbed some of the force of my collision. The
bike and I were sent bouncing down the interstate together. The car we hit took off across the median, over
the northbound lanes, and out into the field on the east
side of the highway.

While I was still in the air, I could see Karl soaring
above and a little ahead of me. He was slowly rotating,
much like a circus aerialist. I'm not sure how many times
he spun before hitting the concrete, but I'm told he flew
through the air around one hundred feet before he
landed. At the point of impact, he must have been traveling close to sixty miles per hour.

The bike and I spun down the interstate side by side, it
on its side and me alternately on my back and belly and
rear. I kept thinking to myself, "What kind of a person

19

stops his car in the middle of the interstate?" Meanwhile I was picking up images of Karl going down the road ahead of me.

Handstanding.

Rolling.

Bouncing and cartwheeling.

He just kept landing and bouncing and landing and bouncing. I'm reasonably certain that at this point he was still conscious, because he was managing to get his hands down to cushion most of his falls and his body seemed to be under some semblance of control.

But then I think he must have broken his arm, because he lost control and his head hit the pavement quite hard. The helmet exploded. Disintegrated. That must have been the blow that did the most serious damage, because from that time on his whole body was limp. The blow must have knocked him out.

There were then at least two terrible bounces with his whole body crashing and snapping violently, like a rag doll doubled over and spun. He was bent backward, and his head and his feet landed at almost the same spot. I'm sure that was when his back was broken and his spine severed.

After that, his body kept rolling and bouncing down the pavement. He finally came to a stop on the center line, crosswise, with about half of his body in each lane. He was lying some 100 to 150 feet beyond where the motorcycle and I came to a stop.

My first thought was that somebody would come over that hill and run right over both of us. I tried to get up, but both my legs were broken, above and below the knees. I tried to get my helmet off. I kept reaching for the snap, and then I realized that my right hand was bent back to my elbow and was useless. My left arm wasn't that much better.

By now there were people running over to both of us.

"Get somebody on the other side of the hill. We've got to stop that traffic, or they'll get Karl again!"

"Somebody's already doing it," a man assured me. He looked like he was going to be sick and sat down on the grass beside me.

The boy who was driving the car in front of the semi-trailor had pulled his car off the road into the right side ditch. "Don't worry about the other guy," I heard him say to the people who were helping me. "He's already dead."

I didn't bother to argue with him. I could see Karl's head in a pool of blood, all split open and ugly.

I soon realized that my pants were all torn up the seams on the insides of my legs. I couldn't remember if I had put on my underpants that morning, but I didn't think so. Two elderly ladies who had come over to see if they could help me asked what they could do.

"You can cover me up."

They used their hankies. Maybe it was the most humanitarian thing anybody did for me all that day.

The pool of gas I was lying in was beginning to make me very uncomfortable. It was getting in my cuts and scrapes, but nobody wanted to move me.

"We don't want to hurt you," they said.

They probably were right, but it seemed funny at the time. Here I was, busted up from head to toe, and these people were worrying about hurting me!

I soon heard sirens in the distance. One of them sounded much closer than the others. I could barely see it, but a highway patrol car was coming up the median at a furious rate of speed. He might have been doing ninety. There were cars everywhere by now.

I later learned that his name was Shiffler. State Patrolman Wayne Shiffler. Wherever you are, sir, hats off to you. You saved my buddy's life.

I'd never seen a cop who looked like he could run, but this one came out of his car at full gallop and took charge right away. I swear the car was still doing at least ten miles an hour when he came out of it, running with a bottle of oxygen in each hand.

I'd never thought I could be so happy to see a cop! I started screaming. "Get him first! Get his teeth out! You'll have to get them out so he doesn't suffocate."

In my shock I had forgotten about his plate until that moment. Shiffler pulled out Karl's teeth and gave him oxygen right away. I'm sure that saved Karl's life.

By this time the ambulance was pulling to a stop. Patrolman Shiffler came over and said, "Son, your friend's still alive. I don't know how, but he is. We're going to take him over to Methodist Hospital right away. I don't think we can take the time to get you on a stretcher, too. There'll be another ambulance here immediately."

I could already hear another siren in the distance.

"Sure, I can wait."

I wasn't trying to be a hero. I was in shock, and the pain hadn't fully hit my system yet.

The strange thing is that I was conscious through it all and never did black out. The whole scene seemed very unreal. I could still smell the musty odor of the car trunk, and everything seemed far away. Detached. My head was still ringing with the sound of the crash, and I had to concentrate to hear what people were saying.

The attendants picked Karl up in one of those magnesium apparatuses that slide together underneath a person. They scooped him up, ran to the ambulance, and were away before I realized what they had done.

By now they were helping the driver of the car back across the interstate. I could hardly believe my eyes. She was just a kid! I found out later that she was a sixteen-year-old girl from forty miles west of Minneapolis. She had been driving into the city for her first job interview.

It was also her first time on an interstate highway. She had become confused and had made the wrong turn. She told Patrolman Shiffler that she had tried to cross on the median, but the wooden posts blocking the way had confused her. So she had just sat there trying to decide what to do, until we came along and decided the matter for her.

She kept saying how sorry she was. She was crying and hysterical. At first I almost felt sorry for her. Then I thought of Karl all busted up and maybe dead, and my broken bones and the chunks of my flesh spread out over 350 feet of concrete, and I got very angry and began to yell at her.

"Shut up! You hear me, shut up! You've busted up me and my friend, and I don't want to hear how sorry you are!"

They put both of us into the same ambulance. By then I was starting to feel some real pain, and I alternated gritting my teeth and holding my breath all the way to the hospital.

CHAPTER 4

Not Expected to Live

●

MONTY KRIZAN:

We'd had so much fun together, Karl and me. And now this. I couldn't believe that that big, crazy, fun-loving guy could be dead.

When we arrived at Methodist Hospital, I could hear the ambulance attendants swearing about the news people blocking their way. The word had gotten out almost instantly that a Viking had been badly hurt and was in the emergency room at Methodist. Inside, I could also hear all the commotion taking place in one of the stalls. I assumed that was where they had Karl since a whole crew of doctors and nurses were busily going in and out.

They put me in a stall at the other end of the room. I really don't remember where they put the girl. I could hear Karl grunting and moaning.

"At least he isn't dead!" I said to myself.

I could tell from their voices that they were having a difficult time holding him down. Even with his broken back, crushed ribs, and broken arms and legs, they could barely contain him. At times you could hear him gasping. I kept saying to myself, "Atta boy, Karl. Give 'em hell! Give 'em hell!"

I had just become used to my surroundings when the room exploded with excitement. Karl's respirator had begun to malfunction, so he and his whole retinue were moved quickly into the next available stall. Evidently, the doctors did a wonderful job on him, because I could hear through the curtains the low murmurs about how critical his condition was. I later found out that his heart stopped beating a couple of times that night, and they had to shock him to get it going again.

It was a while before a doctor and nurse arrived and began to work on me. By then Patrolman Shiffler had been there to get my side of the story, and my wife, Marianne, had made it to the hospital.

I had holes in my skin, and chunks of flesh were torn out of my stomach, legs, and rear end where I had slid along the pavement. They began scrubbing out the holes in my stomach first.

I wanted something for the pain since I was very uncomfortable by then, though still in shock. The extremely severe pain would come later. I think my concern for Karl numbed my pain somewhat, too. I kept listening to the doctors and nurses discussing his condition, and I could hear him groaning and moaning.

With the washing over and under medication I was put in an upstairs ward. I didn't know then that I wouldn't have surgery on my bones for two more days, or I might have really been frantic. They said something about avoiding surgery during shock if it was at all possible.

I was still slipping in and out of never-never land when somebody turned on the television. The local news was playing, and I heard the newscaster saying, "Karl Kassulke, veteran strong safety of the Minnesota Vikings, was severely injured in a motorcycle-automobile accident on Interstate 494 today. . . . He's not expected to live. . . ."

Not expected to live!

I began yelling for the nurse. She came to my bed, and I got very demanding. I wasn't going to lie in bed not knowing what was happening to Karl. "You can either take me down to the intensive care unit yourself, or you can get one of his doctors up here to tell me what's going on."

"We'll get someone right down to your room."

Well, nobody came, and even when Marianne would go down to check, nobody would tell her anything. They wouldn't even let her into his room.

This scene was repeated several times, and it was only when Karl's older sister, Carmen, came to see me the next day that I found out anything. She had flown up with the rest of the family from Milwaukee.

"Monty, I don't know. He has woke up a couple of times, but each time he began swearing like I'd never heard him swear before. . . . violently, and real full of hate. Then he'd just drift off . . . ," she said between tears.

But at least I knew he was still alive. God knows he was tough enough to take about anything!

About two days later they finally let me go down to the intensive care unit. I was in my wheelchair, and he was strapped flat on his back to a large board.

There were large pools of sweat on his chest and belly. The board was soaked. His whole body was still in shock, and it trembled most of the time. Every few minutes he would shake and twitch violently, and the nurse would rush over and watch his pulse rate carefully.

I sat there for well over an hour, and every once in a while Karl would wake up in a rage and begin to mutter.

"Dirty, stupid bastards. . . ." He would then swear viciously. Karl wasn't above swearing now and then, but this was beyond anything I'd ever heard from him before. Then he'd slip back into his sleep. I found out later that this is a fairly common behavior pattern for people whose bodily functions have been violently interrupted.

I remember sitting there and thinking to myself, "You know, Monty. Anybody who can cuss like that after what he's been through is tough enough to make it."

Maybe I was whistling in the dark. But that was all I had.

CHAPTER 5

Roots

●

They say you're supposed to start a story where it begins. For me that's my family—big Otto and Leona, and us five kids. How do you explain any family to an outsider? In my case you just say it was fun, warm, and loving. Sometimes it was even a little crazy.

Both my parents grew up close to where we lived in West Milwaukee, Wisconsin. Dad was an athlete there and later played basketball at the University of Wisconsin in the mid-thirties. He was a good athlete and strong; if the Depression hadn't created so many problems for his father's business, he could have stayed all four years. As it was, he only played for two years and then had to come home and help his father at his bar.

Mom loved each of us five kids dearly. It seemed like she was always available for a talk, and most of her work was directed at helping us with whatever needed to be done. There was never a surplus of money. We had enough, and we certainly weren't "poor." But with five kids to clothe and feed, she had to watch things closely.

If any one memory of Mom stands out, it is her burnt meals. Mom was a very good cook. But people came first with her, and every so often she would be helping a neighbor or doing something with one of us kids and forget that she had a meal on the stove. Dad used to call our home "the firehouse." We'd all have a laugh when he said that, but nobody really minded. How could we when if it wasn't one of us she was helping, it probably would be the next time!

We did things together as a family. Mom, Dad, Willard, Carmen, Christine, Kathleen, and I would get around the kitchen table and sing old songs, like "Hi Lillie, Hi Lillie, Hi

Lo" or "She'll Be Comin' 'Round the Mountain." The reper-
toire was nearly endless, and it's stayed with me all these
years. We also played games together, though everybody
insisted that they had to watch me closely. Supposedly I had a
tendency to cheat!

Some of our best times together occurred when we went on
vacation. While we were growing up, Dad worked at the
Harnischfager plant in West Milwaukee. They made P & H
heavy construction equipment, and Dad helped to assemble
the large bridge crane. He would get one week of vacation a
year, and we made the best of it.

On that special Friday Dad and Mom would get up around
3:00 in the morning to get packed. That way we could take off
at 3:30 in the afternoon as soon as dad got off work. Packing
and loading all that stuff on top of the car in the middle of the
night made for some exciting moments. Inevitably, Dad
would just get it all packed up, and somebody would have
something to put in or take out of a suitcase. On these occa-
sions I learned some of my more colorful vocabulary!

We sang as we rode, taking turns picking our favorites. By
the time we arrived at Lake Lucerne, we would have sung
them all so many times that it really didn't make much
difference who had picked which song. But we still had to
take turns. "To let the girls have a chance," as Mom put it.

One year we took off for vacation over the Fourth of July
weekend. I remember it was cold and rainy, and we forgot to
pack our warm clothes. We had to stop on the way and buy
some sweatshirts, which used up a lot of our savings. Then
another problem arose. Most of the gas stations were closed,
and the ones that weren't closed were low on gas because of
the holiday. It got later and later and still we hadn't found
gas. Mom and Dad were afraid we'd have to stay in the car all
night—an idea that pleased all of us kids. Finally we saw a
light up ahead, which turned out to be one of those gas station
and bar combinations that are so common in rural Wisconsin.
It was raining very heavily, and when Dad jumped out of the
car, he stepped in water over the tops of his shoes. At first the

owner must have thought Dad had come to drink, because he kept shaking his head and saying the place was closed. Then, when he saw Mom and the rest of us kids, he let Dad buy a full tank.

Mom and Dad were relieved, though we kids weren't so sure. We didn't know what we'd missed. Dad told us that sleeping overnight in a car was one of those things in life that if you miss it, you don't miss anything at all. That gave us something to ponder.

Vacation meant fishing, and at all times of the day and night. We used a cabin owned by a friend of Dad's. They had cleared the land together. We called the lake "Stone Lake,' after the huge stones and boulders that lined the floor of the lake. One of our first jobs each year was to push the boulders and rocks down into the deep water to make more room for swimming. Eventually we cleared enough to make a nice swimming beach. The water was cold and clear.

One of the best times to fish was after supper. At first, one of us would always be dropping something or making too much noise. But once we got the hang of it, Dad, Willard, and I developed a good system.

We took turns. One of us would row the boat up and down the shore while the other two would run out their lines. Once one of us had a fish on the line, the other would have to reel in his own line and help the one with the fish. The rower would stop rowing, hand the net to the one helping, and then hold the light while they netted the fish. The one who caught the fish would then become the rower, and we'd change off like that until we'd all had enough.

It wasn't the perfect system, I suppose, but it worked! And it also taught us the value of teamwork.

Some days we would go through the channel into Riley Lake. The channel was so shallow that we had to take our shoes off, jump into the water, and walk the boat through it. It was great fishing, though, because it was secluded and few people knew about it.

Other days we would swim across the lake. Carmen and

Dad would row the boat, and Willard and I would swim. Willard was not a strong swimmer, though he was good in most sports. But I could swim the three and a half miles easily. The water was icy, and once Willard got so cold we had to pour brandy in him to get him warmed enough to finish. We teased him that some people would do anything for a drink.

Willard never quite saw the humor in that!

Willard and I were close in many ways and played most sports together. He was older and larger than I was, but I played with him and his friends anyway. They tolerated me.

My mother still laughs about the story of the little boy in Wauwatosa, Wisconsin, whose dad had been one of Willard's friends. Anyway, many years later Tom Kneusel's five-year-old boy, Ronald, found out that his dad had played football with a Minnesota Viking when he was a kid.

"Was he really good?"

"Naw, he was just a little kid who used to get in the way."

So much for fame and glory!

Willard and I worked at odd jobs in the neighborhood—like mowing lawns and shoveling snow—to earn our spending money. I must have been about nine when I bought my first baseball glove. I had been telling Mom how much I wanted a glove, so she persuaded my grandpa and some of the neighbors to let me help them with extra projects.

I finally got about ten dollars together, and Mom and I went downtown. I'm left-handed, so my choices were a little more limited. After looking for some time, I finally found the perfect glove. Mom took one look at the price tag and with a sick expression handed it to me. $17.00.

"Do you see what this thing costs?" she gasped. But true to form, she just dug down in her own purse and pulled out the rest of the money. And that was that.

We both agreed that it was a good thing that left-handers didn't need left-footed shoes, too!

When I began junior high school, I joined the Catholic Youth Organization so I could play football. The public schools didn't have football in the junior high schools, so I joined the group from St. Florian's Church in our neighborhood. Since the coach didn't want anyone to know I was a ringer, he changed my name to O'Kassulke—which was crude. But it worked.

I always wanted to play football. I think I inherited that desire from my dad, who told me about his school days when they didn't have much equipment and practiced on a cinder patch. Their games were in Southside Stadium, and the field there was mostly sparse grass on clay. When it rained, they would play "tackle and slide," as he called it. It was so bad that they would shower with their uniforms on to try to get rid of the clay.

Our equipment was a little better than his, but not by much. And there wasn't enough for all of us. Each boy was supposed to bring his own, but I knew that our family couldn't afford such an expense. So I told Dad that the coach had said I could use what they had at St. Florian's.

What I used was the old equipment nobody else wanted. It seemed to work fine, since I never did get hurt—at least not out on the field. My dad, a good Lutheran, was a little curious about what I was doing over at St. Florian's. One day he got off work early to see how I was coming along. When he saw me out there with an old, flappy leather helmet and no shoulder pads, he grabbed me, took me off the field, and administered the only real injury I ever received in CYO football!

I wasn't so successful in basketball. The coaches told me that I kept forgetting it wasn't football, so I joined the swimming team.

We held our meets in the Waukesha pool, which must be the hottest, most humid place on earth. I did fairly well in swimming and even won some races. The family always came to watch me swim, and I felt sorry for them sitting there in that heat with all their clothes on.

Willard and I spent much of our free time down along the

railroad tracks that ran not too far from where we lived. In laying the tracks through that area, the railroad had cut out a gully through the woods we called "Treetown." When we were older, we would even hop a slow-moving train in the morning and ride it north, sometimes as far as Fond du Lac. Then in the afternoon we'd catch another one and head on home.

Most of the boys in the neighborhood hung out at Treetown at some time or other. It was full of places to hide and all sorts of interesting animals.

I've always liked reptiles, and one time I picked up about a dozen grass snakes and brought them home to show Mom. She was washing clothes, and when I pulled one out of my pocket to show it to her, she got so excited that she knocked it out of my hands into the rinse tub. She made me take them all back.

I'm sure that there were a few players in the National Football League who doubted it, but I am a gentle person at heart. I've always liked children and small animals. That love has gotten me into trouble more than once, even when I was a child.

A number of large grain elevators stood in the neighborhood where I lived. Once I brought home a baby mouse I had found down by the elevators. It was in the late morning, and everyone was busy with his own work, so I fixed up a place for him down in the corner of the basement. I used an old shoebox and some rags from the rag bin. After supper I proudly took the family downstairs to see my pet mouse.

Dad took one look and started shouting. "Out! Out! Get that rat out of my house!"

How was I supposed to know?

I enjoyed helping my mother around the house, especially in the kitchen. If any of my friends ever thought it made me a sissy, they never said anything about it. When I was younger, I especially liked helping Mom bake bread. We'd get it all out on the table, and Willard and I would fight over who got to punch the dough. To this day I insist that my apple pie and cheesecake are as good as anybody's.

When I was in seventh grade, I decided to become a musician. First I took up drums and cymbals. The junior high band concert in which I played is a favorite joke in our family, but I still think it's too much to ask a seventh grade boy to stand around counting forty-two measures between cymbal crashes! My family came to see me. There they were out in the audience, all lined up in a row. There I was, counting myself dizzy. Crash! Bang! Count . . . . 41, two, three, four; 42, two, three, four; 43, two, three, four. Crash!

Willard and Carmen sat through the whole thing, and I could see them snickering to each other every time I smacked the cymbals. Mom and Dad looked real proud, but somehow I couldn't see how anybody could get too excited over their kid being able to count to forty-four and smash his hands together.

By the time ninth grade rolled around, I had had it with the cymbals. My next experiment was the tuba. Nobody else was playing the tuba, and I figured it was my best shot at playing first chair. I lasted one day. The people living upstairs said I was driving them crazy, and Dad said I'd have to practice in the garage. And that was the end of my career as a musician.

Baseball was a large part of my life then, too. It was a real treat when I was able to go to the Milwaukee County Stadium. Today's Atlanta Braves were the Milwaukee Braves then, and when I was in high school, I became a vendor at their games.

I probably made more money selling pop, peanuts, and other snacks than at any other job I had as a kid. My favorite location was the mezzanine, the closer to home plate the better. Sitting there and in the expensive box seats around home plate were the people who not only bought more food, but would even tip.

After I had worked there for one summer, Willard's partner quit, so Willard and I worked together. The secret was to work real hard and sell big. The team that had the best night would get to choose where they sold at the next game.

We fought to keep our spot.

The championship years were the best for me. Working in the World Series was as exciting to me then as playing in the Super Bowl would be fifteen years later. I was still too young to sell beer, but I ran around madly peddling pop, peanuts, snow cones, and ice cream bars. With my laugh and my loud voice, everybody knew where I was. By the time each summer was over, I had managed to save quite a good sum of money.

Mom was never too happy about my working at the stadium, although she put up with it. She claimed that I was bringing home cockroaches and all kinds of bugs. I never noticed any, but every time she saw a bug around the house, she would start screaming about the cockroaches at the stadium. Then she would fumigate the whole house, and for days after that whenever we worked a game, we'd have to take our clothes off outside before she'd let us in.

Nobody can be as scared of bugs as my mother is. To this day the people who know me well want to know about the tricks I pulled on her with bugs. There weren't any. I was never really afraid of anybody on a football field. But there was no point in riling up Mom with cockroaches! Sometimes the price for a laugh is just too high!

All in all, I grew up in a wonderful, happy home. My brother and sisters were my best friends. Our parents loved us all fiercely. We fought, laughed, fished, cooked, ate, slept, and worked together.

It was a good place to learn what it means to be a part of a team.

And me? I was just that little guy next door who wanted to play football with the big kids.

CHAPTER 6

O'Kassulke

●

I got my chance to play with the big guys when I went to college.

Before that I played for West Milwaukee High School. We were the smallest school in the Suburban Conference, and the large schools from West Allis, Waukesha, and Hale beat us up pretty badly. As a result, I played with injuries much of the time.

In my senior year West had its best team in years. It was the first season we had been over .500 in a long time, and we ended up losing only four games.

Shortly after Christmas my coach, Ray Sonnenberg, asked me to stay after school and talk. He had played for Marquette University during their great years. I think he was Marquette's last All-American in football.

"Karl," he asked me, "have you thought about going to college?"

"Sure, coach. But how am I going to do it? I don't have enough money to do it on my own, and my folks can't help me that much. Besides, I'm not exactly hot copy in the *Journal* sports pages. Nobody's going to give me a scholarship."

"Well, I know, Karl. But I've been talking to Lisle Blackbourn over at Marquette, and he says he might give you a look. Would you be interested?"

Interested? I'd grown up almost in the shadow of the place! Except for the University of Wisconsin, I couldn't think of any place I'd rather go.

So a few days later I went down to see Coach Blackbourn. Since he had coached at Marquette earlier in his career and was successful, the school was hoping that he'd be able to revive their fortunes once again.

Coach Blackbourn was cordial. But several days later Coach Sonnenberg informed me that Marquette had given their last scholarship to somebody from one of the big schools in Chicago.

In the meantime, the University of Wisconsin at Stevens Point had contacted me and offered a football scholarship. Since no other school was interested, I decided that I'd try it. At least I'd be playing football, and that was what I wanted more than anything else.

That summer I worked at the Milwaukee County Zoo and the stadium. One night I got home from a Braves' game, and Mom and Dad were sitting around the kitchen table talking quietly. When I came through the door, I knew that something was wrong.

"They say that you need to send them seven hundred dollars, Karl," Dad said. "I thought you told me you had a scholarship."

"Well, I do, Dad."

I couldn't believe my ears, but I had to believe my eyes. There it was in black and white: Send your $700 right away, or we'll give your room to someone else.

The next morning I went over to show Coach Sonnenberg the letter.

"What do you make of this?"

"I don't know, Karl. There must be a mistake. Let's call them."

He talked to Stevens Point for a long time, but when he hung up the phone, Coach Sonnenberg looked frustrated.

"I don't know what's going on. But I'm sure that scholarship was supposed to be for everything. They say it's just for tuition and books."

Where was I going to get the money?

I probably could have scraped it together, but what then? There wouldn't have been anything left over for food or clothes. Or girls.

Coach Sonnenberg told me to wait. He wanted to talk to some coaches he knew at other colleges. I didn't find it out for several years, but he really twisted Coach Blackbourn's arm—told him I was the greatest college prospect he'd ever coached, and he'd never forgive himself for passing up somebody who'd be as good as I would be. Laid the whole guilt trip on him.

Looking back, it seems rather funny. I mean, West Milwaukee had not produced many big-time college football players, but Sonnenberg was in there pitching and shoveling for all he was worth. Besides, I really hadn't played that much in high school. My injuries had kept me from playing up to my potential.

Coach Blackbourn must have had a sense of humor, though. He said, "All right. I'll take another look at him."

One of the boys to whom Marquette had offered a partial scholarship had just turned down their offer, so something was at least available. Coach Blackbourn had intended to give it to a big fullback from somewhere in Michigan. "But if it's that big a deal to you, Ray, you can tell your boy he's got a scholarship!"

Well, a partial something is better than a full nothing. I was able to eat and sleep at home, and I loved it. The preseason training was even better than I had hoped. Up in the morning. Calisthenics. A light workout. Skull sessions with the coaches. Lunch. Conditioning drills. Contact.

Lots of contact.

Later, Coach Blackbourn said that it was during the contact drills that I made the freshman team. We had a big lineman named Joe Miller who weighed in at about 230. I weighed no more than 182 with my cleats full of mud.

The drill called for one running back and one defensive man to line up on the ten yard line. The offensive man had to take a hand-off from the quarterback and try to get to the goal line before the defensive player could stop him.

I already knew that I was faster than Joe and could run around him. So when they handed me the ball, I went right at him instead. Five times. And I knocked him flat and scored all five times!

I made the freshman team that day.

When my grandfather found out that I was going to go to Marquette, he was furious. He kept saying, "Why do you want to go there? That's a Catholic school. Pretty soon you'll be marrying a Catholic girl. You'll see." He was a hard-nosed, old-style Lutheran who never stopped complaining about me going to a Catholic school.

I dated a girl from Denver my freshman year. And she was Catholic. Her family was well-to-do and had sent her out to Marquette so she could go to a Catholic school. She was supposed to meet a good Catholic boy and get married. Needless to say, her family wasn't too excited about their daughter dating a "Protestant," as they called me.

Jane kept telling me all year long how wonderful Denver was. When she went back home for the summer, I decided to see if the city was really all that great. Just before fall practice began, Mike Kohler, another friend, and I picked up a delivery car from a rental agency. We were going to drive it out to Denver for them.

Dad kept telling me it was stupid, but we did it anyway. Halfway there the carburetor went haywire, and we used up all our food money to get it fixed. We barely made it to Denver. To add insult to injury, when I got out there Jane told me that she had another boyfriend and her folks weren't going to let her come back to Marquette.

So there I was, stranded in Denver. Broke and jilted. I wired Dad for money, and he went down to the bank for me. I hadn't told him that I'd taken most of it out to get to Denver, and he was infuriated. He sent just enough for a bus ticket.

He was still angry when I got to Milwaukee. He was waiting at the depot.

"I ought to beat your stupid head in!" He kept yelling at me. "That's the dumbest thing I've ever seen you do, Karl. And you've done some real stupid things!"

I was relieved that he never actually hit me. He never had, and I didn't think he would. But I was still anxious because when you're a college football player, how do you explain to your friends about getting your block knocked off by your dad?

And he probably could have done it!

We started the 1960 season with a bang, which was surprising since Marquette had done so poorly for so long that few people even bothered to come to the games. We beat Villanova 23–12 in the first game and College of the Pacific 20–0 in the second. Like my freshman season, I played very little in either game. Just some kick-offs and punt returns.

Then came the University of Wisconsin. Since Marquette was an Independent and Wisconsin was in the Big Ten, this game meant a lot more to us than it did to them. I'm sure they regarded us as more of a nuisance than anything, but for us it was our one shot at the big time.

We played them pretty even for three quarters but fell apart in the fourth quarter and lost. Until a couple of passes were dropped and fumbles lost, it was a close game. Still I was elated. I had caught four passes, one for a touchdown from my halfback slot. And I had run and blocked well.

I had gotten my chance to play because the two men ahead of me had been injured the week before. Early in the first quarter I broke a bone in my left hand. I didn't say anything about it to the coach until the game was over.

After the game, Coach Blackbourn told me that I had done so well I was the starting right halfback until somebody could take it away from me.

The team doctor was almost that somebody. On Monday they operated on my left hand and put a steel plate in above the knuckles. I played the rest of the season with it that way.

One of the priests who travelled with the team kept patting me on the back and trying to shake my hand. He was telling me how excited he was about my game.

"You're some German Irishman, aren't you?"

"Yeah, just call me O'Kassulke!" It was the CYO all over again!

After the Wisconsin game the season went downhill real fast. We won 13–12 against Boston College, but we lost the rest, and the season ended on a dismal note.

On a cold Friday morning, December 9th, Coach Blackbourn called me on the phone and told me that there would be a special meeting for the team later that morning. I think we were all there at least a half hour early. Having been finished with football for a couple of weeks by then, we all wondered aloud why the meeting was called.

"I bet he's quitting." It was one of the freshmen.

"After that season, I feel like quitting."

The door opened, and Coach Blackbourn entered. We quieted down as he walked to the front of the room, his face ashen.

"Gentlemen," he said. "This afternoon the university will announce that it's dropping football."

CHAPTER 7

Cowboy

●

Drop football! After sixty-eight years of football tradition, it was like closing down the school. Never! We all began to argue and shout at once.

"Silence!"

We were silent.

"You must have a thousand questions. So do I. But I can't answer any of them right now. I just finished talking with Father O'Donnell myself, and I don't know what's going to happen. Let me say this, though. We will do everything we can to find every one of you a school where you can play. But we'll have to talk about it later."

I couldn't believe it. No football. I would be the starting right halfback next year on a team that wouldn't even exist. Still, Coach Blackbourn had said something about helping us find other schools. I hoped mine wouldn't be another Stevens Point.

As a freshman, I had had a half scholarship. But as a sophomore I'd had a full one, so I was pleased when all the schools that contacted me offered me full-ride programs. I had scored touchdowns against both Big Ten teams we had played, Wisconsin and Indiana; and they were the first to call me. After them were Iowa, Iowa State, what is now University of Northern Iowa, Nebraska, and Drake.

I didn't have anything specific against the schools I turned down—indeed, there were many good reasons for going to each of them. Finally, though, I narrowed the choice to Iowa State and Drake.

Bus Mertes was the reason I went to Drake. First, he offered me a guaranteed scholarship, no matter what happened to me. Then he went that extra step to make me feel wanted. Maybe being at a small school forces coaches to do the extra things, but in Bus's case it just came naturally.

One incident stands out especially strong in my memory. When Bus first contacted me he really tried to sell me on Drake. He pointed out the excellent academic program, the good relationship with the people of Des Moines, all the pretty girls on campus.

Then he went into high gear. "Besides, Karl, even though Drake isn't a religious school, I'm a Catholic, too. And it's important that a good Catholic boy like you have the right kinds of influences when he goes away from home. You know what I mean?"

"But, coach . . ."

"Now, wait a minute, Karl. Let me finish. I'm a Catholic, and several of the boys on the team are Catholic. Des Moines has some fine Catholic churches. Why, there's one almost on the campus."

"But Bus . . ." By this time I was having a hard time keeping my face straight.

"I'm serious, Karl. You'll really enjoy Des Moines, and I'll see to it that you . . ."

"Wait a minute, coach. I'm not a Catholic. I'm a Lutheran. And I have a brother who's going to be a Lutheran minister."

Bus hardly missed a beat.

"Well, we've got some great Lutheran churches in Des Moines, too. And a couple of our coaches are Lutherans. . . . "

All Drake athletes were assigned sponsors, usually Bulldog Club members or Des Moines citizens who enjoyed Drake athletics. Mine was Ed Vilemek. He owned a radio–TV business, and I was able to help him install new equipment and make deliveries. The money I earned helped out on clothes and my social life.

We had a 5–4 record that first year. It was a good team, and I think we were better than our record showed. The next year we were 8–2 with virtually the same players and a tougher schedule.

That 1962 season was the most exciting one I had ever

played. In 1961 I had picked up the nickname "Cowboy," mostly because of my bowed legs. I had made a few long runs, and Tony Cordero of the *Register* and *Tribune* stuck me with the title. I thought it was strange. I'd never ridden a horse in all my life, but here I was "galloping" across the turf at Drake Stadium.

Much of the publicity and attention was centered around me that year. That was more than a little unfair, since football is a team sport and several other players also received post-season honors. Quarterback Terry Zang, for instance, was drafted by the Green Bay Packers and guard Jerry Bartol was drafted by the Los Angeles Rams. We had a very good line. They moved a lot of people out of my way and made some of my best runs possible. The play of linemen is often overlooked in football, and more than one clubhouse conversation has emphasized that very point. What we had was a very good team. And it was that teamwork that made us winners.

Like Marquette, Drake has a big intra-state rival: Iowa State. Losing to them was especially unpleasant. In my senior year they were pregame favorites by more than two touchdowns. We didn't let that get us down and came out with fire in our eyes. We moved the ball well before petering out at the 37 yard line. But then, because of a low pass from center, the punt went only two yards and Iowa State got the ball on the 35. They went the length of the field to score.

It was our turn in the second period. Jim Evangelista, our captain, powered it in from the two for Drake's first touchdown against the Cyclones in five years.

Dave Hoppmann scored for Iowa State in the final quarter, and we ended up losing. We had a good chance to win at the end of the game but fumbled on the Iowa State twenty with about three minutes left. Still, it was not a bad defeat; we could have beaten them if a couple more breaks had gone our way.

After the game Clay Stapleton, head coach at Iowa State, was very gracious to us. The newspapers quoted him as saying that they won the game only because they had more first-line players than we did, not because their players were better.

BUS MERTES (now a coach with the Minnesota Vikings):

Karl was the best back to come to Drake since the legendary Johnny Bright. He was certainly the best I ever coached on the college level. I always called him the "coach's player" for any team. He was the total team man.

He set the modern record for kickoff returns with a ninety-five yarder against Idaho State, and all he could talk about was the beautiful blocking his teammates gave him. There were two all-American backfield men in Iowa at about the same time as Karl, Hoppmann of Iowa State and Ferguson at Iowa. I wouldn't have traded Karl for either of them. Not only was he that good, but his influence on the team was impossible to measure. Nobody ever enjoyed a practical joke better than him, but nobody ever worked harder for the team, either.

One incident comes especially to mind. During his senior year he got tremendous press coverage. Hardly a week would go by without someone wanting to interview him. I don't remember which paper it was, but the reporter was right in the middle of his interview with Karl, and Karl said, "Hey, I'm sorry, but I better go. The guys will think I'm dogging it."

The funny thing was that he could have stayed there talking to that reporter through the whole practice, and the players wouldn't have resented him. He got the publicity, and they didn't mind. Lots of times a star is resented by his teammates, but not Karl. I've never seen a star player who had his teammates pulling for him the way they did for Karl.

And the wonderful thing about Karl is that he never showed any sign of it going to his head.

I was fortunate to receive several honors that year. First I was named Most Valuable Player at Drake for the second time. We had many good football players on that team, and several others could have been chosen for the award just as easily. I was overjoyed, and grateful.

I was totally surprised by the second honor, though.

I was in the library studying one afternoon when one of the library assistants told me that Bus Mertes wanted to see me right away. So I went down Twenty-sixth Street to the athletic offices just east of the stadium. I could tell something was up when I walked in the door. Several people were grinning broadly.

"Karl," the secretary smiled. "Coach Mertes wants to see you in his office."

Bus was sitting behind his desk, and he came around it to shake my hand. The smile on his sun-lined face was as broad as I'd ever seen it.

"Karl, you've just been chosen to play in the Blue-Gray game in Montgomery, Alabama, on December 29. I trust that my acceptance for you meets with your approval?"

It was one of those rare moments when I had to search for words. All I could say was, "I presume they want me to play for the Blues."

I had always hoped I would get a chance to play professional football, and so I was especially excited about this honor. Maybe I'd be drafted after all. Drake, being a small school, didn't get a lot of national attention, and I'd wondered if I would get a chance. Now I probably would.

Professional football wasn't my only dream. I had done quite well academically at Drake, preparing to teach history and coach at the high school level. I still wanted to do that, but the dream of playing for the pros—for a few years at least—was very strong.

The Blue–Gray game was a great experience. Meeting legendary coaches like Bob Devaney of Nebraska and Bump Elliot of Michigan was inspiring. And playing on the same field as the men I had been reading about for four years was an even greater thrill. I played against some of them for much of my NFL career.

We won the game, and I got in on my share of the action. The only dark side to the game was that I injured my arm and was taken to St. Margaret's Hospital in Montgomery. A Dr. Parker took a look at it. He had me move my fingers, twist the wrist, and raise and lower my fist. Everything seemed to work properly. He wanted to order an x-ray, but I was in a hurry to get to Chicago. I was meeting my girlfriend there, and we were driving up to Milwaukee to visit my parents.

By the time we got to Milwaukee my arm was killing me.

We were going to go out to eat that night at the La Joy, a delightful Chinese restaurant in Milwaukee. It had snowed that day, and because of the snow that had been pushed to the curb, I didn't see the fire hydrant alongside my car. All I knew was that my arm was hurting terribly, and I was glad to find an easy parking place in front of the restaurant.

When we came back to the car after dinner, I saw a little envelope on the windshield. I didn't even look at it. It looked like a religious pamphlet of some sort, so I just tore it up and threw it on the street.

That was a mistake. I had driven my parents' car that night, and they didn't know anything about the parking ticket. A five-dollar parking ticket is bad enough, but the notice of "Payment Delinquent" carried a considerably larger sum attached to it.

By that time I had decided to stop by St. Mary's Hospital. The x-ray showed a broken arm. I wasn't all that surprised.

While I was at Drake, I gained a reputation as a free spirit. It wasn't that I was always looking for a practical joke. They had a way of finding me! But I must admit that I enjoyed improvising on a good one. And I didn't always possess the ability to distinguish between a good joke and something quite dangerous—even dangerous to me.

One of the ways I kept in shape during the off season was to work out with the weights and run on the track in Drake

Fieldhouse. One day one of my teammates came up to me with a grin on his face. Two others were tagging along.

"Kassulke, these guys want to bet me ten dollars that you're not dumb enough to jump off the balcony into the sand pit for a quarter."

It looked like a "Have you stopped beating your wife?" type of question to me. But I chose to see it as a challenge to my courage. Off to the balcony I went.

Drake Fieldhouse can best be described as an old barn. Like many of the fieldhouses of its era, the fans watched basketball games and other athletic events from a balcony that extends around the whole facility. When the intercollegiate programs were moved to larger arenas, a running track was installed on the balcony.

I went up to the balcony and jumped unthinkingly into the pit.

Stunned by the shock, I sat there for a minute or two before I got up. I had thought the sand would cushion my fall more than it did. But I did collect my quarter, and my friend got his ten dollars.

As I walked into class the next morning, the professor was talking about the stupid thing he had seen in the fieldhouse the previous afternoon.

"I was working out in the fieldhouse yesterday, and some dumbbell from the football team jumped off the balcony into the sand pit. He could have broken his leg or his hip for a lousy two bits!"

I got the message!

One afternoon I was working out in the fieldhouse when a group of sorority touchball teams came in to practice. I didn't pay a lot of attention to them because it was a fairly common thing at Drake for varsity and intramural athletes to work out at the same time. Then I noticed a quiet, brown-haired girl playing on one of the teams. It was the first time I'd ever seen her.

I motioned one of my friends over.

"Jim. You see that girl over there?"

"Which one? There're only thirty of them."

"Aw, come on! The brunette with her hair pulled up on top of her head."

"Yeah, I see who you mean."

"Well, I think she's new around here. You know, she really ought to have someone to watch out for her. Don't you think? You never know what some of these guys might try with a cute little freshman like that."

"Sure, Karl. I've been looking for a date for the dance Saturday night. I'll go over and get acquainted."

"Shut up, you bum! I want you to go over and subtly find out her name for me. O.K.? You do know what the word subtle means, don't you?"

"Huh!"

He was on his way. I went back to my sit-ups.

I hadn't been at it for three minutes when I heard my name being called.

"Hey, Kassulke!"

"What?"

I stood up to see who was calling me.

"Her name's Jan Thatcher!"

CHAPTER 8

Rookie

●

We were married the next July.

It was a beautiful wedding at the Methodist church in Boone, Iowa. The bridesmaids all wore matching pastel long, flowing gowns. The guys wore tuxedos. Most of my buddies from Drake were there, as were several friends from the Boone Merchants softball team I played with that summer.

With Jan being the only girl in the family, her mother and father went all out to make the wedding a grand event. There were cakes, cookies, sandwiches—just about every kind of food imaginable. My dad got the job of making the homemade ice cream. To this day he swears that it took him days to recover from the effort of handcranking all that ice cream. I maintain that it was the party afterward that did him in.

In spite of the fact that I had to be on my best behavior, the reception was very enjoyable. It was good to see my family again. Willard was studying to be a minister, and it had been a long time since we had been together.

I had drifted away from the religious commitments of my youth, and Willard was concerned about me. After he talked with me about it, I agreed that getting married was a good reason to make a new start. Later, Jan and I would make sporadic efforts to get involved in church but never really worked at it. It just didn't seem worth the effort.

By the time the reception was finished, my football and softball friends had had enough formal partying. They excused themselves and headed for the fairgrounds, where they had rented a place to conduct a reception more suitable to their tastes.

Jan and I left on our honeymoon.

Since the wedding and reception had been held at the

Methodist church, my friends had been unable to bring their beer to the reception. So they elected my dad to be the host of their own party. I think they chose the right person.

When Dad got there, the place was in pandemonium. One of the guys had tried to tap the keg and hadn't known enough to tighten the tap. Beer was shooting in a geyser all the way to the ceiling, and everybody was laughing and reaching for what they could get with their own cups. Tuxes and dresses alike were splattered. Being from Milwaukee, Dad knew just what to do. By the time he got the thing tapped right, half the beer was lost.

Everyone from out of town was staying at the Holiday Inn at Ames. Several of the local people, who weren't even staying there, decided to continue the party in Ames. Mom still laughs when she tells how the guys climbed up the diving board and, one after another, dove off the three meter board into the swimming pool, still wearing their tuxedos.

I had been drafted by the Detroit Lions as their eleventh-round choice in April, but I never really had a chance there. I had received most of my publicity in college for my offensive play, but I always thought I was a better defensive player. I enjoyed the slam-bang style of ball that went with playing defense. Detroit had spotted this interest and ability and had drafted me as a defensive back. They intended to look at me as a cornerback.

At the time Detroit had one of the best defensive secondaries in football. Veterans like Bruce Mahar and Denny LeBeaux were among the best in the league, and they had good second-string replacements. To make matters worse, cornerback is a position in the professional game that requires more speed than I had.

So Jan and I left Boone, Iowa, for Detroit right after the wedding with our old car and a rented trailer. In Detroit Jan had to live cooped up in a hotel while I tried to make the team. She had already enrolled at Wayne State University in Detroit for the fall semester. I was proud of her ambition and drive.

Being a rookie is never easy. Some of the greatest stars ever to play the game barely survived training camp as rookies. Some men with great potential never do. But trying to break into a veteran-studded backfield as a rookie was even worse.

There was no encouragement from the Detroit veterans, as opposed to what I would later find in Minnesota. The harrassment went beyond the normal obnoxious hazing of rookies that takes place in all camps. It was brutal. And, in my opinion, had I been the greatest player ever to play the game—which I wasn't—I wouldn't have stood a chance to make that team.

One incident summed it all up for me.

By the time of the first intrasquad game I was pretty hostile toward some of the vets. When I got my chance, I'd make it up to them by putting a little "extra" effort on my tackles. In the process, I caught Terry Barr with a good lick, and he was injured.

I could tell that something was wrong the next day. It didn't take long to find out what it was. On about the second or third contact play, one of the men playing in the defensive secondary with me came charging in and speared me in the back with his helmet while I was making the tackle.

It seemed a little strange, but accidents happen on the football field. So I ignored it. It happened again. By the time practice was over, I had two broken teeth, two black eyes, several cuts and bruises, and a broken nose.

I got the message.

We played Cleveland in the annual Detroit *Free Press* charities game at Tiger Stadium that weekend. Because of my injuries, I was in no condition to play much football.

On Monday I was cut.

Later that week I was sitting in the training camp office waiting for my last check from the Lions. The people in the front office had been very nice to me, and I saw no reason to be surly. I was joking with the secretaries and enjoying myself.

George Wilson's secretary came out of his office and walked over to me.

"Coach Wilson would like to see you in his office, Karl."

"Thanks!"

I thought to myself, "Maybe they've changed their minds!"

I walked into his office, and he smiled and shook my hand.

"Karl, I'm real sorry things worked out like they did. But I think you'll make it somewhere. As a matter of fact, I've got an old friend on the line, and he'd like to talk to you."

"Sure, coach." He handed me the phone.

"Hello, this is Karl Kassulke."

"Hello, Karl. This is Norm Van Brocklin. Coach of the Minnesota Vikings. We've been looking at you for a long time and think you might fit in here real well. Would you like to come out and join us?"

"Have football will travel!"

CHAPTER 9

Hunkie

●

Five minutes earlier I had been laughing and joking with some new friends because it seemed like a better thing to do than cry. Now I had hope. I was going to get another chance to keep doing the one job in this world I most wanted to do.

Everybody wished me luck. They were all smiles and kept patting me on the back and telling me they thought I'd do well. All I could think of was getting back to the hotel and telling Jan.

Later that night, we agreed that it would be best if she were to go back to Boone and stay with her parents until we found out if I made the Vikings' team. The Vikings held their training camp in Bemidji, Minnesota, about two hundred miles north of Minneapolis, and there wouldn't be anything for Jan to do there. Besides, we were broke.

The Vikings had played San Francisco at Portland the first weekend of preseason play and had decided to stay on the West Coast for the Los Angeles game the second week. Ed Sharockman had been injured during the San Francisco game, and they needed someone to fill in for him at cornerback. That was one position where they were quite thin in personnel, and they needed someone fast. I played a little that week, but not much. And it was awesome for my first time to be playing on the same field as the best in the game.

The Vikings also enjoyed hazing their rookies. It wasn't brutal, like it had been in Detroit. It was rough, and sometimes violent. But there was some sense to it.

Coach Van Brocklin gave the same speech to every group of rookies.

"You are rookies. That means that you are part of the scum of the earth. You are not yet professional football players.

You are still attempting to enter the National Football League. It is an elite group of men. A fraternity. And like any fraternity, there is an initiation involved. This camp is your initiation. That means that if a veteran tells you to shine his shoes, you shine his shoes. If he tells you to carry his bags, you carry his bags. If he tells you to carry his meal to the table, you will do that, too. The same is true if he tells you to kiss his behind. You just get down there and do it, boy!

"If you make this team, then you are in the fraternity. You will then be a part of the most elite group of men in the world. One game. And then you are a veteran."

Training camp was no picnic. We were up at seven, and over at the field by nine to get taped for practice. If it was hot, we'd be in shoulder pads and shorts in the morning. From 10:00 to 11:30 we ran every kind of running drill imaginable. It seemed like they'd never let us stop.

Lunch would be at noon, usually with time off afterwards. Then it was back to get taped up again at 2:00. At 3:00 the contact drills commenced. This was the heavy part of the day's work, and we were in full uniform for the one-on-one drills, tackling practice, and scrimmages. Once the pre-season games started, the schedule was less strenuous toward the end of the week.

Practice ended at about 4:30, and we'd go to the Dutchess Bar to have a beer. Supper was at 6:00, followed by a meeting from 7:00 to 9:00 or so. We usually had from 9:30 to 11:00 to go out and have some more beers.

Sunday was free time. Some of the players went to a church in the area, but most of us were tired and had all we could do to get our personal chores done and get ready for the next week.

A lot of people think football players are stupid. I suppose that we do have our share of slow thinkers, but professional football demands a great deal of intelligence. Much of a football player's time is actually spent in "school," either in training camp or during the regular season. Generally, our schooling consisted of films and talking about what we had seen, or done, on film. We also talked about what was going to happen on the practice field the next day, and the coaches tried to show us how each practice fit into the whole Vikings' system.

For the defense that meant starting with the essential defense and then working on the second, third, fourth, and so on as the camp progressed. As players were cut and as veterans from other teams arrived, we refined these defenses with all the variations the coaches could devise. Sometimes these variations were first suggested by a player who had seen something on the films, or who realized that another approach to a problem might work better.

Once we had been in camp for awhile, we would tease the coaches about the films we were watching. It always started out with the razzing.

"Hey, coach. What's the flick for tonight? *Lolita?*"

"Forget it, buddy. Green Bay Packers."

"Boo!" (From everywhere.)

"Always the Packers."

"As soon as you guys can beat the Packers, then we'll show you something else."

"What's with the Packers anyway? You coaches are always talking about them."

"How about a little skin flick, coach? We've been cooped up here without our wives all this time, and we need a break."

Eventually, the razzing would become a little more intense.

"Oh, coach! Could we see another Green Bay film tonight?"

"No, I want Los Angeles. Give me the Rams or give me death."

It never made any difference. We got what they wanted us to have, confirming the golden rule: "Thems that's got the gold makes the rules."

One of the traditions we were establishing was the post-skull-session party at a local tavern. Later, in Mankato, we would settle on one bar: Metler's. In Bemidji it was the Dutchess.

Van Brocklin didn't want us mixing with the locals, especially those of the female gender. He forbade our frequenting the local drinking establishments. The reason we were able to get by with going to the Dutchess was because it was so run down that none of the coaches would ever go there.

One night we were all out there when several of us decided to stay after curfew. Norm was out of camp. I think there had been some family matter he was taking care of. Anyway, Rip Hawkins had been elected defensive team captain, and he decided to make a unilateral pronouncement.

"I'm the captain of this ship of state, and I'm responsible for you guys. Let's stay out."

Later, we all agreed that the fact that he'd had a few too many had corrupted his usual good judgment.

I was hardly one to argue. There was a certain logic to his idea. After all, the coach was gone, and who else but your captain should be in charge? After several beers it made a lot of sense.

When we got back to the dorm, it was locked and the whole crew began pounding on the door and yelling and singing:

> Hooray for Norman,
> He's a hero at last.
> Hooray for Norman,
> He's become a horse's ass.

Needless to say, it didn't work out too well. Seven or eight of us were fined $500 each. I remember Tarkenton, Hawkins, Gordy Smith, and Larry Vargo; but I'm certain there were more. When I called Jan to explain why the next check would be a little short, she didn't seem to appreciate the camaraderie developing in camp. She kept talking about how maybe some of the other guys could afford it, but we sure couldn't.

"Besides, Karl, you haven't even made the team!"

"I know, Jan. But it was such a wonderful party."

Most of my playing time was on special teams that year. Kickoffs and punt returns were my specialty, not running the ball. Knocking down the guy who had it was what I did best. My role was that of a glamorized kamikaze pilot, sacrificing my body for the team.

John Campbell and I were both rookies that year, and we developed our own competition to see who would get to the ballcarrier first. We bet ten dollars on every play, and by the end of the season we were about even.

The idea behind special teams play is that if you really hustle down the field, you might get a good shot at the ballcarrier before he gets his balance and starts to fly. For someone like myself, here was the opportunity to cut loose. As long as I had played football I had enjoyed the violent contact. And at Minnesota I got my chance to play contact football all the time.

It soon became apparent that I was not fast enough to play the corner in professional ball. Before long the Vikings switched me to strong side safety, where I played throughout my career.

The strong side safety lines up on the same side of the ball as the tight end and is responsible for turning in all the runs on his side of the field. He also defenses the tight end on passing plays. I was comfortable in that position, because I could utilize my enthusiasm for hard tackling to its fullest.

When training camp broke, I was still with the team. By then Norm Van Brocklin had taken a liking to my aggressiveness on special teams and defense, and he gave me plenty of encouragement. He had also given me a nickname: "Hunkie."

Norm knew that I was German, but he liked to tease me by calling me Polish and "dumb Polack." I still don't know where he got the idea that I was Polish, but his insults made me angry at first. I later realized that that was probably his motive. He always told me that I played better when I was angry.

"Hunkie" meant "dumb." I decided to make the best of it by

turning the name-calling into a game and beating him at it. Little things, like whenever I took my salt tablets or any other dressing room concoction, were a chance to go into my routine for Norm.

"OOOOOHHH! The power. The strength. Growing. Surging through my veins. Exploding through my muscles. Power! HUNKIE POWER!"

Before long Norm was suggesting that I tone down the "hunkie" stuff!

Combined with my laugh, which with its high-pitched honking could unnerve most anyone, I think that for at least a while I had him convinced that I was crazy. Maybe that was why we got along so well.

I roomed with Ed Sharockman that year. We were great friends, but he just couldn't handle my laugh—or my snoring.

ED SHAROCKMAN:

Karl was an early morning and late night freak. He'd go down the hall and sit in on the late night bull sessions. I'd get to bed early so I could catch up on the sleep I'd missed the night before while he was snoring like a freight train roaring through our room.

Then, wham! Hunkie would bang open the door, laughing that awful laugh, and proceed to tell me everything that had been said. He'd laugh himself silly at his own jokes.

Then, after he'd got me wide awake . . . zzzz! He'd be off to never-never land in a second and keep me awake half the night again with that awful snoring.

———————

Bill McGrane, the Vikings' public relations director, came up to me one day and asked me why I laughed "in" instead of "out" while exhaling like most people do.

"Karl, I've never seen anybody who does it like that. Why?"

"What do you mean, 'Why?' All us Hunkies are great laughers. Hunkies are great at everything!"

When I was still quite new to professional football, people would ask me why I was playing defense. I had made my reputation in college as a running back, and no amount of explaining how I really was not good enough to be a running back or that I really enjoyed the defensive backfield would convince them. Soon I learned to tell the following story.

There was an old prospector who had come to town to pick up his monthly supplies and had wandered into the saloon for a few beers. Unfortunately, there was also a tough-guy gunslinger in the saloon, and in the prospector he saw a chance to provide some entertainment for himself.

"Dance!" he ordered, pulling out both guns and peppering the prospector's boots. "Now, I want you to keep it up while I reload!"

Instead, the prospector reached into his bedroll and pulled out his ten-gauge, double-barrelled shotgun. As he pointed it right between the surprised gunslinger's eyes, he smiled.

"Now, sonny. Have you ever kissed a stinkin', dirty, slobbering old mule on the lips?"

The cowboy just looked at that gun, swallowed hard, and weakly spoke.

"Nope. But I always wanted to."

Folks, a fella's got to make the most of his opportunities.

CHAPTER 10

Scrambling for Our Lives

●

We were flaky. There was no doubt about it.

We were a new team still trying to discover ourselves. And, for some reason or other, some strong personalities gravitated our way. Winston. Warwick. Hackbart. Dickson. Mackbee. Tarkenton. Marshall. Eller. I'd like to include Kassulke on that list.

We were all fighters.

People used to kid Fran Tarkenton about being a scrambler. The truth was that he was running for his life. That's how we all played—like we were scrambling for our lives.

Carl Eller, our defensive end, was fast enough to catch running backs from behind. At 250 pounds he must have destroyed the ego of more than one running back. Someone once asked him how fast he was in the hundred-yard dash.

"I don't know," he answered. "I never had to chase a quarterback that far."

That's what we were like in those early years. Unpredictable.

One of the men who contributed to that special flavor was Dale Hackbart. He signed on in 1965 as a free agent after playing five or six years with the Redskins. Being a veteran safety, he was a threat to my job, and I wasn't sure how to handle it. Soon, though, we were the best of friends, especially after I discovered that he played free safety, rather than strong safety. We quickly got ourselves scheduled as roommates.

Hackbart was one of those unique players who came our way. He readily admitted that he was a "marginal" player. I don't mean he didn't earn every cent anybody ever paid him to play football. It's just that if he hadn't been Mr. Determination, I don't think he'd have made it.

That's probably why both of us made it. The line between the good and the best is a very fine one at the professional level. I always felt it was the men who wanted to play badly enough who eventually made it in the NFL. The Hacker wanted to play.

One incident stands out in my mind. When the Hacker joined the Vikings in 1965, he was a six-year veteran and didn't have to come to rookie camp. That meant he had no warning about Dave Osborn, from the University of North Dakota, who didn't look all that tough but who soon proved he was.

It was a one-on-one drill, a variation on the one used in colleges all over the nation. A defender, usually a linebacker or defensive back, is placed on the goal line and a running back is placed at the five. The back can run back and forth all he wants since the defender cannot cross the goal line; but once he crosses the five, he's fair game. Obviously the runner is trying to get to the end zone, and the defender must stop him before he gets there. The winner gets to go back in line, and the loser has to stay on the field until he can beat someone. It is a very effective drill for evaluating how tough a player is. It can also be very embarrassing.

None of the veterans had heard of Ozzie. Many of us had never even heard of North Dakota before we came to the Vikings. The coaches gave Ozzie the ball, and the next thing we saw was Hackbart lying on his back and Osborn standing in the end zone.

"Wait a minute. Give the ball back to the rookie. He won't do that twice."

He did.

"Give it to him again!"

Would you believe three times?

Osborn, a real shy guy, looked almost embarrassed.

Hackbart walked up to him and said, "Osborn, I don't know

who you are or where you come from, but you are sure some tough dude. You should make this team!" That's the kind of guy the Hacker was. Tough. And generous. He welcomed Osborn before he made the team himself.

After he stopped the next rookie, Hack came over and asked the rest of us veterans who this Osborn kid was. "I've never had anybody run over me like that before."

Bill Brown answered him. "I don't know. He's just some kid who showed up out of 'Can-Do,' North Dakota."

We found out later that week that he had been knocking people down like that during rookie camp, too. He was serious about everything, the kind of guy who would be in bed by ten o'clock. Whenever the coaches came around to do their bed check on us, Ozzie was always in bed sleeping.

It was the Hacker who began to perfect our harrassment of the rookies. We had always made our rookies do ridiculous things. That was how we tested their fortitude. Every meal the rookies would have to stand at attention, loudly introduce themselves, and sing their school song at the top of their voices before they ate.

It was unbelieveable. Two-hundred-sixty-pound men were standing with their hands over their hearts singing their alma mater. If they didn't know it, they had to hold on to their crotch and sing the school fight song. Some of them didn't know either one. Many were so embarrassed that they couldn't sing even if they knew the words. Those guys were the ones we went to work on.

"You don't know your school song? Shame on you, rookie. Shame. Does anybody here know it so we can teach it to the rookie? No? Shame! Four years of college and he doesn't even know that! What song *do* you know?"

A tune would be named, and then the sentence would fall: The offender had to stand on his chair and sing it, accompanied by gyrations of varying degrees of impropriety. The whole team would hoot and boo and throw food to show their appreciation. When somebody couldn't handle it, the harrassment became even worse and never let up.

One young man from Nebraska, I believe, was especially shy. He was a good offensive guard, but all the hazing finally got to him. He would get sick out on the field just thinking about the ceremonies at supper, and he began coming to the dining room early. That way he could be done and gone before we got there.

This went on for two or three days, but then we missed him and Jim Marshall made the announcement. "No food will be served rookies until the time posted for each meal." The rookie was there the next meal, and we made him get up and sing.

He finally just walked out of camp.

He went over to the Indian reservation on the other side of Lake Bemidji and stayed there for five or six days without anybody knowing where he was. He hadn't taken any clothes with him, so one day he sneaked back into camp while we were practicing. Jim Finks, the general manager, talked him into coming back.

He did. For one day.

That night we made him sing his school song. The next day the linemen gave him a real rough time out on the practice field, and he walked out of camp for good and went home. The sad thing is that he would have made a fine offensive guard. On the other hand, maybe the pressure of pro ball would have been too much for him to handle.

Not every rookie put up with our hazing, though. One of them probably owed his job to refusing to take it.

Earsell Mackbee was older than the usual rookie. He had played on a fine Utah State team and had gone directly into the army out of college. After two tours of duty he felt he had taken enough harrassment and was justified in not putting up with any from us. "You can take your school songs and shove 'em," he would say. "You can drink your own beer, too. I don't have to do it just because one of you clowns wants to make me look stupid. And if you don't like it, then try to do something about it."

We veterans thought he was being obnoxious. After all, when we were rookies we had thought it was stupid, too—but we had done it, and we thought he owed it to us. So we harrassed him on the field and at the table and even roughed him up a little. Because he took it and gave it back, Earsell soon became one of the most respected men on the team. That didn't mean he was belligerent. There would be days when he would go along and sing, and there would be days when he wouldn't. But it was Earsell who decided, not us. And in the end it paid off for him.

Norm Van Brocklin also was a fighter, and he liked fighters. Naturally, he enjoyed Earsell, and he gave him his chance. In time he became a valuable member of our defensive unit.

After he had made the team, Earsell developed a rather unorthodox way of warming up at practice. Paul Dickson was a quiet, gentle guy who read philosophy and poetry. He also grumbled and growled a lot. Van Brocklin alternately called him "The Philosopher" and "Happy." Earsell would get out on the practice field and begin to limber up his legs. Before long he would find Dickson and begin growling at him like a dog.

Even though Paul was ordinarily mild mannered, before long he would be in a rage, screaming that he'd kill Earsell if he got his hands on him. By the time Paul had calmed down, they both were warmed up, laughing at each other, and ready for another day of practice. I always wondered what would have happened if Paul had gotten hold of Earsell while he was still so angry.

Their relationship was symbolic of what those early Vikings teams were all about. Crazy. Flaky. Fiercely proud.

My kind of people.

CHAPTER 11

Till the Coffee Gets Cold

●

The early Vikings were almost an extension of Norm Van Brocklin's personality. Whether it was on the field or in the bars, at home or away—whatever we did, we did to excess, and without full self-control.

Norm had had a brilliant professional career as a player, and he knew all the ways players had found to get around the coaches' rules. He had probably even invented a few new ones himself. He was the kind of person who loved people—really loved them—but you never knew where you stood with him. One minute he'd have his arm around you, and five minutes later he'd be cursing at you.

Also, he had been such a perfectionist when he played that he couldn't understand why players made mistakes. It was almost as if he felt that we stayed awake nights looking for ways to make them. A missed tackle or block, a fumble or dropped pass—any one of them would earn his bitterest wrath as if you had attacked him personally. He saw every mistake as a reflection on his ability to coach. Worse, he seemed to feel they were acts of outright rebellion against him. He never seemed to understand that sometimes the other guy just beats you. You didn't commit an error—he was just better, at least on that one play. One game against the Packers comes to mind quite vividly.

It was early in my career, my second year. The Packers beat us that Sunday 42–11. We all played poorly, but on one play I looked particularly bad. When we looked at the game films on Tuesday, Norm ran that play through five times.

The pass was over the middle to Jerry Kramer, one of the toughest tight ends I ever had to cover. I was still new as a strong side safety; and though I felt comfortable with my coverage of running plays, I was still unsure how to handle the tight end on passes.

I kept wishing I had chosen a seat by the door. Instead I had to keep watching Kramer catching the ball. Me off balance. The stiff arm. And my feet flying out from under me as Kramer hammered down the middle of the field.

By the time this scene had reappeared for the fifth time, Norm could contain himself no more. "Kassulke," he screamed. "When Kramer hit you, you splattered like dog s—— on a sidewalk!" Instantly, the room was filled with screaming and hooting! Candy bar wrappers. Plastic cups. Pop cans, gum, newspapers. You name it. It all came flying my way.

"Coach, I didn't do it on purpose. I just made a mistake. Don't take it so personal. He just made a good move and beat me, and I tried to tackle him too soon."

More laughter.

"Kassulke. This isn't Drake University. It isn't West Milwaukee High School, either. This is the NFL! You do know what the NFL is, don't you?"

"Yes."

"Then play like you know it!"

Three plays later he stopped the films again. And this time he was yelling at Roy Winston.

"Winston, why can't you tackle like Kassulke?"

You have to love a guy like Van Brocklin. Even if you can't understand him.

Norm did more than just yell at us for our mistakes. One of his favorite punishments was making players roll from one end of the field to another. Time after time. After twenty or thirty yards you don't know where you are. It's a little like standing up, spinning around real fast, and trying to run in a straight line. He devised this punishment while we were in training camp in Bemidji. One night he caught some veterans sneaking out to the Dutchess after hours to meet some ladies. His response was to roll the energy out of them. It worked so well that he refined its use for the regular season.

At every practice he would call out the names of the men who would have to roll from end to end and how many "laps" they would have to do. As soon as practice ended, the offenders would line up on one end of Midway Stadium and roll to the other. Whenever we were not one of the people rolling, we would stay and encourage them on their way.

"'Atta way, Moose. Keep going there. Keep it up."

With thirty or so players yelling and jeering, confusion and frustration grew rapidly. More than once somebody would become irritated, and the action would pick up to match the talk! It is hard to roll in a straight line, and it was nearly impossible with everybody yelling and laughing. More than once I found myself rolling toward the goal line, only to realize at the last moment that it was the one where I had started!

Practice was run pretty much according to Norm's personality. He worked us unmercifully in the warm season, but once it got cold, things changed. Norm never did adjust to Minnesota's weather too well. The later in the season it got to be, the shorter the practices became. He walked everywhere with a large cup of coffee in his hand, and we used to say that when the coffee got cold, practice would end.

Norm's unpredictableness was as apparent on the field as off it. No official ever enjoyed having to come over to the bench to talk to him. His language could blister the ears off a sailor. Even though they had to approach him twice a game for the two-minute warning, many officials never came close to where he was at any other time.

In one particular game, he became so upset at a call that he went running out onto the field screaming and cursing. The official had, in my opinion, made a bad call, but Norm didn't help matters any. Instead, he picked up a fifteen-yard penalty for unsportsmanlike conduct. In a rage, Norm chased after the referee, only to be held back by the players. He was so mad that he finally broke away from us, dug into his pockets, pulled out all the change, and threw it in the referee's face.

As a player he had been a fierce and intense competitor. A football genius. And that's the way he coached.

We reacted much the same way. We acted out on the field what was happening on the sidelines. You don't like the Packers? You go out and kill them. Somebody giving you fits? You go out there and knock him senseless. Wild and crazy. Rough and tough. Undisciplined.

It would all change when Bud Grant came.

While Norm was coaching, there was one event we looked forward to every week—"The Bronze Jock" award. Norm had created this award for the person on offense and the person on defense who had made the most violent hit of the game. The hits couldn't be cheap, just bone-jarring.

He had a trophy made out of a bronzed jock. I don't know how he got it manufactured, but it looked real enough to have been one. It was awarded each week during the game film. When we came to the play that earned the award, the projector would be stopped and the award given. We all coveted the bronze jock as a real status symbol.

I got my share.

For some reason Norm liked to pick on Ed Sharockman. Ed pulled the muscles in his legs quite often, especially during the early part of training camp. His having to take it easy for a couple of days drove Norm mad. Finally he decided that Ed needed to see a psychiatrist: No professional football player should go around complaining about sore legs! Griping about that kind of pain sounded sick and effeminate to Norm. It even justified in Norm's mind his nicknaming Ed "Psycho."

So Ed went to see the psychiatrist one afternoon. He returned that night during the team meeting. Norm saw him and started yelling. "Stop the film! Stop the film! Get those lights on!"

It got real quiet. We didn't know what was happening. We hadn't noticed anything terrible on the films, and because

Norm was so unpredictable none of us knew who was going to be the object of his wrath this time.

"Well, Psycho, what did your shrink have to say?"

"Well, coach," Ed answered. "He thinks I'm fine. Now he wants to see you."

When we went on the road, Van Brocklin gave us money for our meals. If it was a Sunday game, we would arrive in town about 3:30 or 4:00 on Saturday afternoon. For Saturday games we'd get there on Friday.

In 1966 we went out to Cleveland to play the Redskins in the doubleheader game that was shown on national television. We were to play in the 6:30 game on Saturday night, and then Cleveland and St. Louis were to play the late game.

Van Brocklin had said, "Karl, you and Rose and Sharockman and Hackbart have made the team. I'm not going to play you very much. Probably not at all. I've got to play these rookies and see what they can do because I've got to make a decision on who to keep."

So we took our meal money and left.

We were staying in downtown Cleveland near the stadium, and we decided to eat at a small Italian restaurant. After a couple of drinks at the bar, I had an announcement to make.

"Gentlemen, since we're not playing tomorrow, we're not going to eat. We're just going to sit here and drink and get nice and mellow."

I must have been a born leader.

So we didn't eat. We drank. And we drank. We got bombed—totally snookered.

George, Ed, Hack, and I walked down the street going from one bar to another. Singing and laughing and spreading Viking cheer everywhere. Hack and I found some five-gallon steel buckets in a construction project along the street. We put one on each foot and proceeded through downtown Cleveland in those buckets, walking into bars, laughing and singing, and having what we thought was a grand time.

I had had far too much to drink, and George and Ed were helping me down the street when we met several of the Redskins. I knew that I wasn't going to have to back up my words the next day, so I wanted to fight them right there.

"Krause, you're the worst safety in the league. Even Hackbart is better than you. We're going to kick the crap out of you tomorrow."

As I said, I had drunk too much.

Fortunately, the Redskins could see how intoxicated I was and just laughed at me. Besides, there were twice as many of them, and they could afford to laugh.

We actually got in by the 11:00 curfew, but Norm must have seen what state we were in. The next morning at breakfast he had an announcement to make.

"Gentlemen. We have some real tough guys on this team. They think they can go out on the town the night before a game and get bombed. We're going to give them the opportunity to see if they can play football tonight. Hackbart, Rose, Sharockman, and Kassulke will play all the way. And they'll play on the special teams, too."

And we did!

We played with terrible hangovers, and it was the worst game I ever played. The fact that I had mouthed off to the Redskins the night before didn't help either, and they took their revenge with relish.

That was the irony of Van Brocklin. He was the kind of guy who probably had broken some rules himself when he played, but he could really put the screws on us. If you could get something by him, you knew you had really accomplished something. Our attitude must have been obvious, because he really did think we were out to get him. And when he caught us breaking his rules, he would go off the deep end. I've never seen anybody so unable to forget a mistake.

On the other hand, Norm had a brilliant football mind, capable of picking out a particular play that could definitely beat a team. He had been a quarterback with the Philadelphia Eagles, and one of the best at that.

Norm had a memory like an elephant and expressing his anger about mistakes didn't make him forget them. One time in 1966, for instance, we were playing in Green Bay. It was a tight game, and I was preparing to go in for a crucial defensive series. He called me over.

"Look, you go out there and stick to Kramer. You hear me? Stick to him! I don't want him running over you like he did that other time."

How on earth could he remember that play two years later in the middle of a tension-packed game? You just never knew when he'd remember something, either good or bad.

I first learned that Norm had quit as coach when Paul Dickson picked me up at my house one morning. I was dumbfounded. He'd always called us a bunch of quitters. "Quitters and losers!" he would scream after a disappointing loss.

"Where'd you hear it?"

"Well, somebody from the *Star and Tribune* called Paul Flatley this morning."

Both Flatley and Dickson disliked Norm. Norm once called Paul "the man caught from behind more times than any player in the history of the NFL," and Paul resented it. He had been the NFL Rookie of the Year, and his own coach making fun of his slowness was too much for him to take.

Norm and Dickson just didn't get along. Period.

We all began to laugh about how good it would be to be rid of Norm.

"I know you're not supposed to love your coach," Hackbart was saying, "but this is too much. I'm sure glad I'll never have to play for him again."

We all agreed.

"I never thought he'd quit! I thought he might can all of us, but him quit?"

"Yeah! But ain't it great! I might even enjoy playing football again."

Paul Dickson was driving; as he stopped at a red light and

turned to look at the Hacker, who was riding shotgun, his face blanched.

"Hey, guys. There's the Dutchman himself."

We rolled down the windows.

"Hey, Norm. How ya doing!"

He had a big smile on his face and just waved at us. The light changed, and he headed the same direction we were going.

As we drove on to Midway Stadium, the conversation took a decidedly different tack.

"Geez! He's headed our way."

"Do you suppose he's going to the stadium?"

"Probably. I bet he's going to clean out his locker."

"He sure didn't look like somebody who was going there to clean out his locker."

"You think he's back?"

"Naaah! He's got to be coming over to get his clothes and clean out his locker."

When we pulled into the lot, Norm was just ahead of us. He drove around the corner and parked in his space. He was smiling as he got out of the car and waved to us as he went into the offices.

We walked into the locker room. It was a zoo.

Jim Marshall was running up to people, grinning and yelling, "Yaaah! He's gone! He's gone!"

Earsell Mackbee was slapping hands and grinning from ear to ear. Two rookies were playing leapfrog around the room and whooping with joy. I hadn't seen such a happy group of Minnesota Vikings for a long time.

"Wait a minute!" It was Dickson. "Wait a minute. We just saw him come in the building and walk down the hall to the meeting room. He might be back."

It got quiet real fast. All of the sudden Stubby Eason, the equipment manager, came in the door. He looked scared, like he didn't want to do what he had been sent to do.

"Fellas," he said. "Norm's back. And he wants you all down in the meeting room."

It was a very quiet, solemn group of Vikings who walked down the hall. We got there and sat down. Somebody coughed.

Norm got up.

"Gentlemen, this is very difficult for me to do. . . . I quit last night, but I'm back. I believe in you and this club. And I'm here to stay."

"You phoney hypocrite!"

It was mild-mannered Paul Dickson. He was on his feet and his face was red with anger.

"How can you stand up in front of us after you've quit when you've always called us a bunch of quitters and losers? And then you've got the guts to tell us you're back with us to stay? Well, I don't want you back. Why don't you just go and let us play football for somebody who hasn't quit on us!"

I could hear several "Yeahs" and "That's rights" around the room. Then it got quiet. Very quiet.

And the Dutchman apologized.

Just like that.

He was very humble about it. It must have taken him a whole week to get back to his old self—screaming and shouting and swearing and insulting everyone right and left. And it wasn't long before he decided to leave for good.

CHAPTER 12

Mr. Discipline

●

Things were totally different under Bud Grant. That doesn't mean he didn't have a sense of humor or didn't enjoy a good time. I've seen those steel-gray eyes dance with delight many times. But he was always under control.

And that control is what he set out to teach us.

In a way I was sad to see Norm go. He was a real genius at designing game plans and offensive formations. In many respects he did more coaching than Bud did. And because his reckless personality and mine were so well-matched, we were drawn toward each other in at least as many ways as we fought. There's still the warmest kind of feeling down inside me for him.

When Bud Grant came south to Minnesota (and I think too many people have forgotten that for Bud Minnesota was the warm country), he first had to teach us self-discipline. Some of the rules he made seemed trite by themselves, yet they were all part of a strategy designed to take a bunch of wild and crazy guys who made a lot of mistakes on the field and mold them into a solid football team that would wear their opponents down and capitalize on their mistakes.

Who would dare to argue with his success?

At the same time, it would also be unfair not to point out that Bud's success was built upon Norm's foundation. Both men played their roles in the development of the great Vikings teams.

For Bud the roles and skills necessary to mesh us into a disciplined team were amazingly varied. He had to be mother, psychiatrist, head coach, father-confessor, financial counselor, and administrator for forty football players used to a sparring partner for a coach.

It wasn't that he disliked our rowdiness or the practical jokes. In fact, he was known to pull a few jokes of his own, but his were very subtle. Bud didn't feel any need to be around to see the consequences of his pranks—knowing that they had worked seemed to be reward enough for him. In fact, it was accepted in camp that if nobody could figure out who had done a trick, one could assume that it originated with Bud until proven otherwise. He encouraged such spontaneous pranks as great tension relievers. He did insist, however, that we not disrupt anyone's personal life or interfere with their ability to play football.

When Bud first came to the Vikings, we were a do-your-own-thing kind of crew. This attitude carried over to both the practice and game fields. On the practice field it expressed itself in the many different gimmicks we had developed for keeping ourselves warm. One of us would wear long underwear. Another would wear special mittens or smear a heating lotion on his skin. There is an unending selection of products available for keeping warm on the football field, and we all had our favorites.

Bud put an end to all of them.

"The more you emphasize the cold, the colder you are going to be. It's as simple as that. So there will be no warming paraphernalia in practice or on the field."

"You've got to be kidding, coach!"

"No, I'm not kidding, Kassulke. Let me tell you a true story to illustrate what I'm talking about."

Thus began Bud's perennial story about the Eskimos and the Distant Early Warning (DEW) line.

He told us how the cold created unbelievable problems for our government when it was building the DEW system. It was so cold in the Arctic regions that the soldiers constructing the line could only work a few minutes at a time before going inside to warm themselves. As a result, three times as many men were needed to build the DEW line as would normally be required.

Then someone got the idea of training Eskimos to run the

machines, and the results were amazing. The Eskimo people could stay out on the machines all day. They never asked to come in until the appointed break times.

In order to study this phenomenon, a group of Eskimo men were sent down to one of our universities. Whatever tests were run, though, there was no measurable physical difference between the two groups of people. The difference was all in their heads.

The Eskimos knew it would be cold and prepared themselves for it mentally. The Americans knew it would be cold and couldn't handle the knowledge.

"Gentlemen, we all know where we are playing football. It's going to be cold here. No two ways about it.

"But we're going to make it work for us. We are going to become so used to the cold that it isn't a factor in our game. We'll let the other team worry about the cold. We'll worry about playing football."

Bud was not one to stop practice when his coffee got cold! In fact, he had a way of making them last longer in freezing weather.

We didn't do too well during his first year—I think we won only three games. Our losing upset him a lot. After all, he'd been a successful coach in Canada and had even won the Gray Cup.

What concerned him more, though, was how we lost. Roughing the passer. Hitting after the whistle. Slugging. Pass interference. Offside. We must have come close to leading the NFL in penalty yards that year. And without a doubt, in terms of penalties that really hurt a team, we won hands down. One play in particular typified the whole season.

Near the end of the first half of our game against Cleveland, Carl Eller and Jim Marshall had broken down the offensive line and were chasing Frank Ryan, the Browns' quarterback, around in his backfield. Out of desperation Frank threw the ball up for grabs in the end zone.

Earsell Mackbee was originally covering Gary Collins, but in the mix-up of the broken play, he lost him. As the ball came down, Collins and Hackbart came through the same area of the end zone, each going in opposite directions. The Hacker stuck his arm out and clotheslined him. In the collision Gary's face guard was smashed. If he hadn't been wearing one, his face would have been severely crushed.

Hack later told me that he had reacted automatically, throwing his arm out without thinking while trying to prevent the touchdown. The really awful part of it was that Gary wasn't even in the play; the ball was thrown into the opposite side of the end zone. With the penalty the Browns got the ball on the one and scored on the last play of the half. They led, 14–10.

Bud was irate at halftime. He began to list the mistakes that had been made. We all had our share, but Hackbart's made him the angriest.

"Hackbart, that interference of yours is the worst I've ever seen. In all my years of football I have never seen anything so stupid. He didn't even have a chance to get to that ball. Not even a remote chance."

He then fined the Hacker $200.

I started to argue. "Bud, we all made mistakes. Let us all chip in."

"No, it's Hackbart's fine, and it will be quietly deducted from his paycheck."

Bud must have thought that we would correct our mistakes if he had us practice more. We first began to notice a change in the middle of the season. Hackbart was the one who called it to my attention.

"Hunkie, what do you think about these practices? Getting a little long, aren't they?"

"Now that you mention it . . . Say, Hack, I've got a great idea."

And so it began.

Usually practice lasted an hour and a half, but we were nearly up to two hours. So the next day when we hit the one hour and fifty-eight minute mark, Hack and I stopped what we were doing and began jumping up and down, yelling, "World record! World record! We just set a world record!"

Then we calmly went back to practice.

Everybody looked at us like we were a little crazy. The next day we went through our little routine at two hours, ten minutes. The next day, at two hours and twenty minutes, and so on.

We even incorporated new features into our routine each day. One day I did cartwheels up and down the sideline. Another time the Hacker brought a party hat and noise-makers.

By the time we hit two hours and fifty-five minutes, Bud came over to where we were standing.

"What in tarnation do you guys think you're doing?"

Bud," I explained. "You know, we've been out here so long these last few weeks, we've been setting practice longevity records every day."

He looked at me with suspicion. "What's the gimmick, Karl?"

"No, I'm serious, Bud. First it was one hour and fifty-eight minutes, then two hours and ten minutes, then two hours and twenty minutes. Then it was . . ."

Bud had walked away, shaking his head and laughing to himself.

He got our number, though. From that day on he would watch the clock himself and keep us out an extra two or three minutes every day.

I think he enjoyed our act. As soon as we were finished, he would dismiss practice. This went on for several days.

One day Ralph Reeve, a sports writer for the St. Paul *Pioneer Dispatch,* was standing on the sidelines when we went into our act. After practice, he came into the locker room and walked over to me.

"Kassulke, what's going on around here? I've been coming to practice for a long time, and I've never seen this shouting and screaming before. What's it all about?"

So I told him. It was in his column the next day.

As I was getting taped the next afternoon, Bob Hollway stuck his head in the door and said, "Karl, I think Bud is looking for you."

I hadn't seen Ralph's column, so I walked into Bud's office rather casually and sat down. I received one of my better lectures from Bud.

"Kassulke, what happens on the practice field and in the locker room stays on the practice field and in the locker room. These reporters come around here angling for stories, and you've got to watch what you say. It's bad public relations for the Vikings if the people of Minneapolis and St. Paul know that I kept you guys out here for two hours, fifty-nine minutes, and thirty-eight seconds. They'll get the idea that we're losing these games on the practice field and not during the game. So knock off this foolishness about new records!"

There are times when it is prudent to take the advice and counsel of one's superiors! And this was one of them.

There was no doubt who was running the show with Bud Grant as coach. While Norm Van Brocklin had let us eat our meals on the road on our own, Bud instituted the team meal. Supper was at 6:00, and everybody was required to attend, even when we played in our own hometown.

On our first trip to Milwaukee we learned what his style of discipline would mean.

We had lost four games and had won none, and the Packers were in first place. When we got to the Holiday Inn downtown, half the team got out of the bus and went directly into a bar. The rest went into the hotel and checked in. I went home to see my parents, but was back by 6:00. Bud had seen the guys go across the street and into the bar, but he didn't say a word about it.

After supper we were always free until about 10:00, when we would all get into one of the rooms and look at the special teams films. From maybe 7:00 until 10:00 we could do as we pleased, so Hackbart, Joe Kapp, and I decided to go out for a drink. Half of the team came along, and Joe taught us how to drink Tequila.

By 10:00 all of us who were drinking were a little under the weather. The coaches crammed us all into a little Holiday Inn room, one of the old kind that barely had enough room for two double beds. There had to be forty guys in that room, all sitting there smoking cigarettes or cigars, or chewing on Clorets to cover their breath.

Still, it smelled like a brewery!

And with all that smoke, it became very difficult to keep our churning stomachs under control. Several players fell asleep during the films, and Carl Eller fell both asleep and off his chair.

Bud just sat there, quietly watching the films and refusing to comment on our condition. I think he enjoyed our discomfort.

We went out the next day and had a great game, beating the Packers 10–7. Our first win.

Our next road trip was to Atlanta. Bud hadn't said anything about the Milwaukee fiasco, but just before the airplane left Minneapolis, he made his announcement.

"If anyone is caught drinking on the night before a game, or even suspected of it, he will be fined $1,000 the very first time. If you want to drink, do it during the week and with moderation. But don't go out of town and get snookered and play a lousy game. If people see you hanging around these bars, then what are they going to think about you?"

That ended that.

Hack and I frequently went hunting together. One fall we found a great hunting spot owned by a friend of the Hacker in the Twin Cities. It was loaded with birds, and every time we went we got our limit—at least Hack did. I usually had a hard time hitting the broadside of a barn. It wasn't long before Bud heard about it.

Hack and I were standing on the sidelines at a Friday

practice one week when Bud came up to us. He was real casual and talked to us out of the corner of his mouth while he was watching practice.

"You guys ever do any hunting?"

"Yup."

"You got any good spots?"

"Yup."

"Uh, you got a good dog?"

"Yup."

We both knew he was fishing for us to ask him to go hunting with us. So we didn't say anything to him, except to give him another "yup" every time he asked us a question.

Finally, he turned around with that smile tugging at the corner of his eyes. I'm sure he was enjoying the moment even more than we were.

"You know, if you were to go hunting tomorrow, I could probably cut practice a little short."

"Yeah? Well, would you like to come hunting with us?"

"Well, thank you. I'd enjoy doing a little hunting with you."

So the next day Bud let practice out early, and Jim Lindsey, Dave Osborn, Mick Tingelhoff, Hackbart, and I—and, of course, Bud—dressed up in our hunting outfits. When we got to the fields he kept telling us, "Now don't walk too much, you guys. I don't want you to walk your legs off for the game. Let the dogs do it."

From then on it became one of Bud's favorite places to hunt.

CHAPTER 13

One Big, Happy Family
●

Bud Grant taught us how to win. But first we had to become a team.

Bud believed that rules and tradition would help make it happen.

He began to lay the rules down.

Smoking only in the restroom, not in the locker room.

No beards.

Sideburns clipped at the ears.

Mustaches ending at the corners of the mouth.

No excuses for being late for anything.

If we broke any of these or the other rules and were caught, we were subject to disquieting disciplinary action.

"It will be quietly deducted from your paycheck," he would say. "You will never miss it!"

Picky? Yes. Effective? Look at his record.

At times it could be aggravating. His rules demanded a lifestyle very different from the one to which we had become accustomed. It was even more difficult to live by his rules when we knew that most other teams weren't. But then, when the year ended, those other teams were sitting at home watching us in the playoffs! That kind of success made it a little easier to live by Bud's rules.

We became a team. And we became friends. We played, fought, and lived together. The Vikings became a big family.

Following every game, win or lose, we'd all get together with our wives or girlfriends at a favorite bar or restaurant. Eventually, the Embassy in Burnsville became our most regular meeting place. Sometimes Jim Marshall would have us over to his home, and sometimes Joe Kapp would throw a party at the La Casa Coronado. Later, Fran Tarkenton would throw them at a country club.

And then we would party. One of the best of those parties was a Halloween ball at the downtown Radisson. Some of the costumes were extremely creative.

I was there by myself, as usual. Jan was extremely busy with her medical studies at the University of Minnesota, and after the births of our two sons, Kurt and Kory, she didn't feel that she could afford to take time for social events with the team. This became a sore spot between us, but she finally persuaded me that she just wasn't comfortable with the "jock" crowd and was too busy to be there anyway. As a result, I usually went to these parties by myself, except for those times when I brought the boys. I always managed to enjoy myself, dressing up as Santa Claus at Christmas and passing out the gifts and acting as host at other times. I wasn't about to let being there by myself spoil my good time, so I always managed to find some other way to contribute to the evening's success.

This evening Hackbart, as usual, was the life of the party. He had come dressed as a prima ballerina, with Bev, his wife, as "her" escort.

You had to see it to believe it. He'd actually found a ballerina's costume, complete with a blonde wig and long stockings for his bowed legs. Slippers, too. After putting apples in a bra he acquired an instant figure! It was a little dramatic, even for the Hacker.

It seemed that his bustline diminished every time I saw him. Then I realized what was happening. Everytime he got hungry, he would pull out an apple, take a bite, and replace it. By the time the evening was over, all he had left were two dried-up apple cores.

We were a close-knit group of people, closer than most teams ever get. When we get together today with some of the old-time players still with the team, they shrug their shoulders and say, "Oh, we just don't share a lot of things together like the old team did." It's too bad, because I think that closeness had much to do with the success we enjoyed on the field.

Joe Kapp's acquisition helped to change the whole character of the team. You couldn't be with Joe for five minutes without knowing that he was a leader.

Joe hadn't been with us very long when Paul Dickson came over to the Hacker and me at practice one day, laughing. "You know, I think that new quarterback is going to be OK."

"What do you mean?"

We were surprised. Paul made his contempt for quarterbacks widely known. He thought they were all sissies, a common opinion among linemen and linebackers.

"Well, Joe and I went to a party over in St. Paul at the Hilton last night. We were sitting there having a couple of drinks, and some guy came in and began to give him a hard time. He was saying things like, 'Kapp, you're the poorest excuse for a quarterback I ever saw!' and 'Why don't you go back to Canada where they play that sissy ball?'

"The next thing I knew, Joe had gotten up from the table and was chasing him around the dining room. He was too quick for Joe, so Joe tried to kick him in the butt, and his shoe came off and landed right on somebody's table.

"Can you believe it! He was going to take on that guy right there in that nice restaurant! He's going to be alright. He's kind of a tough guy. Not a sissy like most quarterbacks."

Whatever Joe Kapp was, it wasn't a sissy. He's the only person I ever saw mess with Lonnie Warwick.

Nobody messed with Lonnie. Not even Carl Eller and Jim Marshall. Once, when we were in training camp, Lonnie went into their room at about 11:00 or 11:30 at night. They had gotten out their big chess board and were playing with the oversized pieces, maybe twelve or fifteen inches tall, that they always used.

Lonnie kicked those chessmen all around and walked out. Carl and Jim didn't say a word. They looked at him like he was crazy, and then looked at each other and shrugged. I thought they would start beating on his head, but they didn't want to mess with him.

Joe Kapp didn't back off at all.

One good example of his willingness to take on Lonnie was after the final home game in 1967. A group of fans who called themselves the Outside Stadium Club made hamburgers and sandwiches for the players after every game, and for a couple of hours or so we would sit around the parking lot with them eating and drinking. Five or six couples sponsored it, and every year after the final home game we'd go over to one of their homes instead of eating at the stadium. They would roast a pig and invite the players and their wives and friends.

There must have been one hundred people there that night. We had lost to Green Bay in the last minute of the game. Joe Kapp had taken the snap from center, and as Larry Bowie, the offensive guard, pulled, he knocked the ball out of Joe's hands. Everybody dove after it, but Green Bay recovered and kicked a thirty-yard field goal. We lost, 30–27.

Kapp and Warwick were in the family room downstairs, arguing about who had lost the game.

Joe said, "I'm responsible. The offense just threw it away."

Warwick would hear none of it.

"Nuts! The defense lost it."

"Aw, come on, Lonnie. You know we dropped the ball in the last minute and gave them that field goal."

"Yeah, but we made more stupid mistakes than ever. They shouldn't even have been close at the end of the game."

Finally they both agreed that there was only one way to decide it. They'd go outside, square off, and fight it out. As they went upstairs, I heard Joe say, "I ain't never whipped a linebacker before."

It was a phenomenal fight. They knocked down a white picket fence and toppled the homemade fireplace in the back yard. Roy Winston, Jim Marshall, and Carl Eller finally got them separated. I think they would have killed each other otherwise.

As it was, both of them had good shiners. Lonnie's wasn't as

serious as Joe's, but it was no joking matter. We had to play
the Bears in Chicago on Sunday, and Joe's eye was so bad that
he couldn't come to practice until Friday.

The next morning we went back over to the house. Lonnie
and Joe both apologized to the host. Lonnie had lost his teeth
in the fight, and we spent an hour and a half walking around
that yard before we found them.

Bud Grant had a long talk with all of us who had been at
the party. "I don't understand you men. You are grown men,
and you ought to be able to take care of your problems. But
that sure wasn't the way to do it. You need to grow up and
learn some self-control."

No screaming. No ranting and raving.

Just a quiet deduction from two paychecks.

I enjoyed giving the news people an opportunity to earn
their living. They were always angling for a story, and I was
known to cooperate.

Once, Tony Parker was interviewing me for his telecast
following a game in which I had made a key interception. He
went through his introduction, telling fans how important it
had been and how I was a great inspiration to the team. Then
he handed the mike to me, obviously hoping for a description
of the play.

"Bless your heart, Tony. It was real sweet of you to say
that!"

"Cut! Kassulke, what are you trying to do to me?"

"Just helping you earn your pay."

"Well, try to be serious, will you, Karl?"

When they begged me like that, I felt sorry for them. So I
gave him the story he wanted.

Ralph Reeves caught up with me in the Detroit airport
after one game. "Karl, will you describe your interception to
me? I'd like to use it in my column."

"Sure."

I switched into my best news commentator, press conference tone of voice. "Here we are in a pass situation. Now,

notice, folks, how they are in the split formation to the short side.

"Now, usually, we play that situation with what we call the 'Sally Force.' But because of the propensity of the Lions to throw the ball to their tight end, we called a 'Blue Force' in which I hold off the crease to the tight end and fade out to the flanker.

"Our stalwarts in the front four gave us their usual fine rush. Landry put the ball in the air without seeing me, and I snared it, tying my all-time record for pass interceptions. Two in two games.

"This elevated me into a mood of elation, since, combined with our overall performance, it is an absolute delight to be a part of this integral win which locks us into a three-way tie for first place in the Central Division, otherwise known as the 'Black and Blue' Division of the NFL.

"Your obedient servant, Karl Kassulke."

He was just staring at me.

Then we both laughed.

CHAPTER 14

Just a Friendly Game

●

I never really forgot my early experience in Detroit.

And I always did well against the Lions. Maybe I was trying to prove a point.

I made that point very clearly during a safety blitz one time when we were playing the Lions. Lonnie had called it. It was the perfect call for a long yardage situation. We wanted to take the wind out of their sails.

Hackbart was supposed to cheat over a little toward my side of the coverage. I was to be a step or two closer to the line of scrimmage than normal. They came out in a spread formation, the line to the right side of the field. Charlie Sanders was spread out just a little more than usual. He wanted to get downfield fast.

Greg Landry never saw it coming. If he had, he could have called an audible at the line. At the very least, he could have had someone pick me up and block me. As it was, I had a straight run of ten to twelve yards right at him before contact.

Wham!

I hit him while his arm was up and his rib cage was wide open. He was totally unprepared for it and lay on the ground for a long time. I still remember thinking that it had been just like tackling practice. He was so still, so easy to hit. It was like hitting the tackling dummy. An opportunity like that just doesn't come along very often. I hadn't meant to hurt him. I just wanted him to have something to think about.

When we saw the films the next week, I had difficulty understanding how he even lived through it. We ran the play back and forth several times, even in slow motion. Landry's head had snapped just like a whip.

To this day people tell me that it was the best hit they've ever seen in football. I would agree, not so much because I made it, but because it was a perfect team play. We masqueraded my blitz perfectly—they never suspected it. They were so surprised that nobody even warned Landry.

DALE HACKBART:

A couple of years after that play a friend of mine was married in St. Louis, and Landry and I were both in the wedding. He said, "Believe me. That was the hardest I was ever hit in all my years of playing football. I crawled off that field, and it took everything I had to get off."

When we played Detroit, I wanted them to remember me. And I wanted them to know that they had made a mistake when they let me go!

But then, hitting is what football is all about—at least it was for me. I loved it. That's why I played it with so much enthusiasm. I felt that the area I was covering belonged to me, and I wanted people to know that when they started fooling around in my territory, they were going to have to pay a price. I like to think that the men who played opposite me remember me that way.

EARSELL MACKBEE:

The defensive backfield had two main defensive calls. "Cora" was the call when the cornerback (me) was responsible for turning the running play inside. "Sally" was the call when it was the safety's responsibility. In all the years I played with the Vikings, not once did Karl call "Cora." It was always "Sally." He took them all. It didn't make any difference how big he was or how much of an All-Pro. Karl stuck his nose in there every time. You could count on him being there to knock somebody down. It wasn't always the ball carrier. It might be a blocker. But he was always there in the thick of it.

DALE HACKBART:

Karl was like a little keg of dynamite that was ready to explode. Every time he hit somebody that's what would happen. Men his size aren't supposed to be able to take on a 265-pound offensive guard, stuff the hole, and stop the play. But the way he impacted when he hit you, he did it time and again.

There was a play against Green Bay that was a typical Kassulke play. Karl had come up on the strong side run and knocked down Jerry Kramer, which was quite a job in itself. Jerry, who had pulled to run interference for Elijah Pitts, weighed 260 to 275 pounds. Pitts, coming around the corner right behind Kramer, and Hunkie just hit him head-on. Helmet on helmet.

Carroll Dale, the outside flanker, had come back to throw a crackback block on Karl, and his head hit the other two. Pitts, Dale, and Karl. They ricocheted off each other like balls on a pool table.

Karl was the only guy who got up. He was a little dizzy, but the others had to be helped off the field.

He always played like that.

In one Detroit game he came off the field with a broken thumb. The Vikings had just acquired a strong safety; he was supposed to be "all world" strong safety or something almost that good. I suppose the Vikings were thinking about Karl's retiring some day.

Karl's thumb was torn back to the wrist, broken and dislocated. All he did was have it set. When he got it back where he wanted it, he taped it up and three plays later put himself back into the game and told this guy to get out.

Later, the kid came up to me and said, "I've been

around this game awhile, but I've never seen anything like that!"

Neither had I. But I told him he'd never played with Karl Kassulke before, either.

———

It could get very rough on the field. It was always rough, but sometimes it was even worse than usual. A good example was a preseason game against San Diego in 1972.

I had intercepted a pass by John Hadl and had proceeded to return the ball. In the course of my runback, Carl Eller turned and popped Hadl with his forearm. This happened just before the play ended, and John had to be helped off the field.

That sort of action isn't uncommon, especially among linemen. Offensive linemen are notorious for using the moments after a completed pass downfield to look up a defensive lineman or linebacker who has been taking "unfair" advantage of them.

Well, everybody got up and began trotting off the field. Carl was strutting off the field toward our side, proud of himself. His back was to the Charger bench. Rick Redman, a San Diego linebacker, had seen what had happened and decided to take matters into his own hands. Across the field he came at full gallop.

The Bench was all yelling, "Moose! Moose! Look out! Look out!"

Moose thought they were congratulating him. He was grinning from ear to ear when Redman clobbered him from behind at full speed. Moose's helmet came off, but he didn't fall down.

Unfortunately for Redman, he fell down himself. Then, like a bunch of ants grabbing a dead worm, eight to ten guys picked him up and dragged him around behind the bench to beat on him. This brought the San Diego team out onto the field, and both teams met at about our hashmark. There followed one of the most amazing brawls I have ever seen on a football field.

Everybody got fined. The NFL has a rule that gives a $250 automatic fine if a person even puts one foot on the field during a fracas, and the league was about $20,000 richer by the time that game was over.

The roughness had actually begun on the opening kickoff. The Hacker had clotheslined San Diego's highly-touted running back from Kansas State, Mike Montgomery, on the opening kickoff. Dale had come down the sideline, cut behind Montgomery's protection and caught him right across the windpipe with his arm. Montgomery must have lain there for five minutes before he regained consciousness.

On our next kickoff the offensive center circled around and hit the Hacker from the back as the play ended. Dale's wind was knocked out, and the tone of the game had been set.

One humorous incident did come out of that game. One of the coaches later said that Bud Grant just stood on the sidelines impassively, arms folded across his chest. One would have thought he was just watching a Wednesday scrimmage.

Finally, he motioned to one of the coaches and said, "Get Page out of there before he kills somebody."

In the locker room after the game Bud chewed us out pretty well.

"I don't want you to talk to the press about this at all. The days of reliving these things in the media are over, and anybody who talks about it publicly will be fined."

When I came out of the locker room, there was Ralph Reeve again.

"Karl, what happened during the fight? What were you doing?"

"Fight? What fight? I'm a football player, not a fighter, and I don't want my name associated with any fights. I plead the Fifth Amendment."

There was a similar fight in Baltimore in 1965 while Norm Van Brocklin was still coach.

Jimmy Orr and Earsell Mackbee began pushing each other around after the official refused to penalize Earsell for interfering with a pass. Hack came over and grabbed Earsell around the shoulders and started to pull him off Jimmy. By then Earsell had gotten in some good licks.

"Earsell, it's Hack."

The Hacker had just gotten Earsell calmed down when Frank Parker (about 6' 7", 290 pounds) came running up behind him and kicked Hack in the chest. We found out later that two of Dale's ribs were broken. By then Marshall, Warwick, Dickson, and I were pounding on Parker. Paul Dickson took a swing at him, missed, and fell on his face. Instead of laughing at this, Parker also kicked him in the ribs. By then, though, Parker had had enough. He took off his helmet and began swinging it wildly. Nobody came near him.

There was a tremendous difference in how the coaches handled the two situations. Norm had loved the 1965 fight. In fact, he firmly believed that getting your own licks in first was the better part of such altercations. Bud played them down and refused to let us continue our fights in the papers.

During the season our schedule was quite predictable. Monday was the day off. Tuesday was for getting the kinks out. Wednesday and Thursday were for hard contact and scrimmage. Friday had less contact. Saturday was more like Tuesday.

On Tuesdays, players from complementary positions on the offensive and defensive teams would work out together. The offensive ends and flankers would run pass patterns against the backs. That way we could all loosen up together in a way that was consistent with how the game was played.

The linemen would play a game they called "grab ass." Most people know it as touch football.

It was a crazy kind of game. The defensive and offensive lines would play against each other, and the rules allowed for a great deal of freedom. The game was more like rugby than football. They'd throw the ball back and forth, passing and lateraling the ball across the field. Throughout, they fought and argued.

"I got ya."

"No, you didn't!"

"Yes, I did. Now bring that ball back here!"

Whistle. The coaches would have to get in the middle and break up the altercation.

Occasionally, "grab ass" would pay off during actual games, as it did on a snowy day in Detroit. Alan Page had blocked a Greg Landry pass up into the air, caught it on the run, and begun to run downfield toward our goal line. Alan couldn't move fast enough to avoid Nick Eddy, who tackled him from behind. Just as he was falling down, Alan flipped the ball behind his back to Jim Marshall, who was running alongside him. Here Alan was, running as hard as he could and falling down, and still he made a perfect pass. Jim caught it on the dead run and went on in to score.

A newspaper reporter was waiting for him at the gate.

"Marshall, that was a phenomenal play. How did you two make it happen?"

"It was easy," Jim answered. "We play grab ass every Tuesday, and we do that pass all the time. As a matter of fact, we practice that very play every week."

They didn't, but it got into the papers anyway!

Saturdays were much like Tuesdays, and I'd often bring my sons Kurt and Kory to the stadium. Because many of us were family men, there were a lot of youngsters in the Viking family. On some Saturdays twenty to twenty-five of the little rascals were running around the locker room and on the field.

Stubby Eason, the equipment manager, inherited them. Until he died recently Stubby was one of those special people who always did the things that weren't required, whether it was for the team or for a player. Unlike most equipment managers, he sorted out equipment and clothes and put them in our lockers so we didn't have to dig through everything when we got to the stadium. He was a master of the little things that mean a lot.

On Saturday mornings he played babysitter to all our kids. He had a way with them. I don't know how he did it, but he kept them from tearing the place, and each other, apart. Every bit of his ingenuity and energy was required to keep up with them.

Kurt, my oldest son, was, and is, a real aggressive athlete. One Saturday Stubby came up to me after practice and said, "Karl, you've got quite a fighter there, don't ya."

"Sure do, Stub."

"Well, tell ya what. Why don't you see if you can get him to hold it down a little. He was wrestling with Doug Davis's boy a couple of weeks ago and they got in a fight over it. Kurt got mad and bit him."

"No foolin'? Well, I'll take care of that."

"Yeah, Karl, but some of the guys were telling me that their kids didn't want to come today because Kurt tackles too much like his dad."

"Well, at least I get some respect from the kids around here!"

Stubby's Saturday chores weren't limited to refereeing the wars on the sidelines and in the locker room. He often ended up being a babysitter, though he was probably more like a benevolent dictator with them than anything else (when they'd let him get by with it!).

Kory, my youngest son at that time, was just a preschooler when he met his Waterloo with Stubby. Kory loved being on the sidelines with the coaches and players and insisted on watching everything. You couldn't pull him away.

But one Saturday the combination of the cold and his not-very-nimble fingers did him in, and he dumped a can of pop in his lap. Stubby knew that Kory would freeze if he didn't get into some dry clothes, so he marched him into the locker room, wet pants and all.

Kory was doubly indignant by the time they got inside, and

when Stubby ordered him to take off his britches, he refused.

"No!"

"Yes!"

"No!"

"Look, Kory. You either take them off so I can put them in the dryer, or I'm going to throw you in there with them on."

Kory's eyes got big as saucers, and then he started to howl. For a long time he wouldn't have much to do with Stubby.

Probably the only part of the game I ever complained about was the special teams. It wasn't that I disliked them; I took great pride in my accomplishments on them. But there were times when I'd become so tired from playing wide open on defense and then running madly up and down the field on kickoffs and returns. By the time a game was over, it was easy to be bushed. So, soon after Bud Grant arrived, I began to kid with him about not going out there every play.

"Come on, Bud," I'd beg. "Please. Please let me off those special teams. I'm a veteran, and it makes me look bad to be playing on them all the time."

"But we want our best athletes on our special teams."

"A lot of good it's going to do either of us when I get hurt. It's dangerous out there when you're tired, and I get tired running up and down that field all day."

"Karl, you're one of the best athletes we've got, and you're going to play on the special teams. You're too important out there not to play all the time."

On and on we went.

I'd talk to the Hacker.

"Yeah, Karl. But he's right."

"What do you mean?"

"Well, Bud obviously respects your ability, otherwise you wouldn't be out there. You should be proud he insists. It's a compliment!"

One Tuesday we were in the meeting room watching the films from Sunday's game. I had been called for clipping on a punt return and was still burned about it. Bud ran the play through three or four times.

The kick. The catch. My block ("Hmmm. It does look a *little* like a clip."), and then the rest of the play.

"Men, do you see what Kassulke did there? He clipped that guy for no good reason."

"Wait a minute, coach. I didn't clip him. He just turned as I threw my block."

Laughter. Half the guys in the room threw something at me.

"Karl, you clipped him fair and square. You should have pulled off your block and let the guy go. It wasn't that important to the play, and you not only cost us a good runback, you cost us fifteen more yards."

"Coach! That's not a clip. He turned his back."

Bud turned off the projector and ran his fingers through his hair. Somebody found the lights.

Bud sighed.

"Karl, if you clip anybody again, I'm going to take you off the special teams."

I couldn't believe my ears!

"Really, coach? You mean it? Will you really take me off the special teams if I clip somebody?"

Bud walked out of the room laughing.

CHAPTER 15

Training Camps and Telegraphs
●

I really enjoyed training camp. Always.

Perhaps that made me different from many of the players. But training camp was the one time of the year when I had only one thing on my mind: football.

Jan was attending the Univerity of Minnesota, studying to be a doctor. As an intern she was terribly busy, beside being on call twenty-four hours a day; and because of that I found myself very busy around the house during the rest of the year. I did much of the cleaning and cooking and helped the boys with their schoolwork.

I also held various off-season jobs each year and made dozens of appearances every year at places all over the Midwest. Earsell Mackbee and I started the Vikings basketball team, which traveled throughout the region, and I had formed a group called Sports Celebrities Incorporated. We booked professional athletes for banquets and other events.

In addition, I became involved in the bar business. A friend had convinced me that it was a sure way to make a lot of money, and with my father's background in it I knew it was worth a try. Eventually, I owned two in southern Minnesota and one in Mason City, Iowa. The work, especially the problems, was enough to keep me busy full-time.

So, in a very real sense, training camp was like a vacation—another crazy Kassulke idea! At any rate, it certainly represented a changing of gears, and I really enjoyed the physically strenuous activity. Other than the soreness in my muscles during the first few days, the adjustment came quickly.

There wasn't a lot of variety, though—drills in the morning, drills in the afternoon, drills all day long. In the morning they were mostly for conditioning and in the afternoon we did our hitting. After the hitting drills came wind sprints and maybe a conditioning drill or two for the men who needed them. I never fell in that category.

Conditioning drills are mostly running. We would run through ropes, stepping faster and higher each time. For us defensive backs, there were a lot of ball drills. The coach would hold the ball in his hand and move us around by the position in which he was holding the ball.

Back, cut right, cut left, cut forward, backward, forward, right, left, forward, left.

Soon it became a blur, and my legs would begin to feel like they were coming loose. Then the coach would throw the ball off into left field somewhere. By the time I'd fetch it and get back to the line, it was all I could do to catch my breath before it was my turn again.

The next drill would be on another field, so we had to run across two fields. The contact work, such as the hamburger drill, showed even more ingenuity.

The hamburger drill got its name from the two tackling dummies the coaches placed about five yards apart on the line of scrimmage. An offensive and a defensive lineman, and a running back and a defensive back were then chosen. The play had to take place between the two dummies. The ball would be given to the running back, who had to use the lineman to run between the two dummies. The defense was supposed to stop him any way it could.

It was brutal.

Then came the same drill with a quarterback and center. This time the dummies were about 3½ yards apart. The quarterback would take the snap and hand it to the back. The back would try to run over or around the defender.

Another favorite was "seven on seven." The offensive team would collide head on with the defensive team, only without linemen. This drill was usually run "live," which meant that as soon as a pass was completed, the defender could tackle the ball carrier.

Then there was one-on-one pass coverage: an offensive back or end running patterns against a defensive back or linebacker. My job was to bump them around a little, knock them off stride, or tackle them if the catch was made.

The offensive and defensive lines would then go one-on-one for pass protection and pass rush. Since the defensive line was rated so highly, it was the offensive linemen's chance to prove how tough they were. The coaches set up a dummy about six or seven yards behind the line of scrimmage, and the offensive linemen had to keep the defender from getting to the dummy. They would beat on each other without mercy.

Often there would be a full-scale scrimmage after these drills. Other times Bud would put the ball on the ten yard line and say, "OK, offense. You've got four plays to get the ball into the end zone, any way you can get the job done."

Anyone who wondered why we hit like we did during games would have known why if they had ever seen us at practice. It was on the practice field that games were won and lost. And it was there that you made a Bud Grant team. Bud said that more than once, "That's how I judge a player."

We always started practice with an exhausting grass drill and stretching exercises. Then Jack Patera would take the defensive linemen over to an area where they did their own grass drill—rolling and crawling, forward and backward, very fast. This was supposed to improve their agility, but any player who has been through a session of Jack Patera's grass drills would seriously question whether it helped anything. If you can't even move when you finish, how could it improve your agility?

One day, while Hack and I were walking by the defensive linemen, Hack began to harrass Patera.

"Jack," Hack said. "You think you're working these defensive linemen hard, but in the evening we sit up in our rooms and they laugh at you. They laugh at you because they're making you think that they're working hard. Huffing and puffing. See that? You should see them in their rooms!

They're huffing and puffing now all right, but they're making a fool out of you."

Jack just smiled. "Hackbart. I want you to get in here and do the drill."

"Ha! You're not my coach. We both know I don't have to."

"Well, come on, Hack. If you think it's so easy and the guys aren't putting out, you get in there."

"Forget it."

"What's the problem here?" It was Bud Grant. He'd come by to see what all the noise was about.

"Bud, I'd like to borrow Hack from the defensive backfield team just a little bit here to run him through this drill."

Bud agreed.

Hack couldn't very well tell Bud what he could do with that drill, so in he went.

Patera was unmerciful. He splattered Hackbart all over that practice field. He told him that he was going to run him until he couldn't get up any more.

All us defensive backs were standing there yelling, "Yeah, Hack. Get up. Go, man go! Do it, boy."

The humiliating thing for him was that the linemen were doing it, too. And they didn't seem to be having that much difficulty.

It was the only time I ever saw the Hacker totally blitzed!

From that time on none of us messed with Patera. Certainly not the Hacker.

The drill I enjoyed the most was what we called the skeleton drill. The offense had the quarterback, ends, and backs. We would have the linebackers and defensive backs. Warwick, Hackbart, and I went head-to-head with the quarterback for a buck an interception, and that led to some exciting innovations.

One day before practice, Hack and I got together with Joe Kapp and Gary Cuozzo and worked out a system to have some fun with Jerry Burns.

Jerry is the Vikings' offensive coordinator and a very disciplined guy. He'd tell his receivers, "Run down here eight yards, fake a turn to the left, turn to the right, and the ball is going to be in this alley."

We worked out a system together so that the quarterbacks would telegraph the next play to Hackbart and me. The one who wasn't throwing the ball would flash the signals, while the other called out the cadence.

The first play was a pass to Gene Washington. We were in a zone where Hack was supposed to cover the deep middle. Gene's play was to run downfield eight yards and curl in under Hack's coverage.

As soon as the ball was snapped, Hack ran right to the spot where Cuozzo was supposed to throw it and intercepted it. Jerry stood in the backfield scratching his head.

On the next play it was Joe's turn to throw. Gary was also in the huddle, and as they broke huddle and came to the line, he flashed the signal.

Tight end. Fifteen yards, sideline.

This time I was supposed to have the deep middle. But as soon as the ball was snapped, I ran to the right place before John Beasley even made his move. Another interception.

This went on for days.

Jerry is a nervous sort of guy, and he must have been dying inside. He finally called time out one day and came over to the defensive side of the line.

"What in the name of the Almighty is going on here? You guys have been messing up my plays for a week now."

"Well, Jerry," I explained, "I can tell you what's going on."

"Well, you better do it fast!"

"It's like this. Your offensive receivers are tipping off the plays."

"What do you mean, 'They're tipping off the plays?'"

"Well, when Beasley's going to run a sideline, he lines up with his head cocked to the right. And when he's going to run a curl, he's got his head cocked to the left."

I explained how each receiver was telegraphing his moves. He was aghast.

"Is that how you guys have been figuring all this out?"

"Sure, Jerry. That's how we've been doing it."

"Oh, no. It can't be true! If this gets out, we'll get blown off the field by everybody!"

He went back into the huddle and chewed out every one of them. He never did get the whole story.

And when we finally got bored with it, he must have breathed a sigh of relief that his receivers had solved their problems.

CHAPTER 16

The Vikings' Relays

●

It was the coaches' responsibility to keep training camp on the move. I took the responsibility of seeing that our free time offered us as much excitement.

I enjoyed the physical activity, the contact, the on-the-field cameraderie of camp. I was always ready to play. But on the other hand, if I had any say in the matter, there would be much more than that.

Much of our spare time was spent in playing pinochle, cribbage, or poker—lots of poker.

I didn't play poker that much. I never did that well and lost interest rather quickly. Hackbart always said that the reason I did so poorly was that I could never bluff. Everybody knew when I had a good hand, or a bad one, just by looking at my face. And when I had a great hand, my laugh would give me away.

The rules were cash only, usually just the money you had on yourself at the time. Bud Grant had noticed how often we played, and one day he had said, "I hope that there isn't any gambling going on around here. It might get to the point that it affects your performance if you're worrying about how much money you are losing."

"Gambling, coach?"

"Aw, come on. We wouldn't do that."

So we kept the stakes low—pennies, nickels, dimes. When Jim Marshall ran out of money one night, we made an exception. In addition to the fact that he was bigger than the rest of us, he'd been in the game for days and we couldn't kick him out. We let him write a check.

Sometimes discretion is the better part of valor. And sometimes a quiet room can keep a coach from knowing the whole story.

Wednesday was the exception to the strict training schedule of drills, workouts, and team meetings. On Wednesday nothing was scheduled after the evening meal, so the hours from 6:00 to 11:00 were free. The coaches used to say they could tell the good guys from the bad on Wednesdays. The good guys went to the movies, and the bad ones went to the bars.

The Hacker and I went to the bars, usually Metler's.

We'd run down to Metler's before supper. And after supper. Sometimes after the team meetings. Sometimes even after curfew.

I had the travel time all worked out, right down to the second. It took four minutes exactly for us to slip out the back door, run down the alley, jump into my car, and tear up the hill to the dorm. In traffic it took five minutes.

One night we had plenty of time. I think it was 1967. The Hacker and I were walking through the alley when I noticed something unusual. It had probably been there all the time, but we had just been running too fast to notice it earlier. Directly behind the rug company stood a whole stack of hollow cardboard tubes. Apparently they had been used for carrying the rugs and carpets and then had been discarded.

"Hack, I've just conceived an idea that even outdoes my frequent brilliant bursts of creative genius."

"Sure, Hunkie."

"Really. You see those tubes over there?" I pointed to the stack. They looked pretty solid and must have been eighteen to twenty feet long.

"Yeah."

"Why don't we have a track meet in the dorm some night?"

"You've had too many beers, Hunkie."

"No, I'm serious. We could go down to the college athletic field and borrow some hurdles and things. And we can use these poles for pole vaulting and . . ."

"Wait a minute! Where are we going to do any pole vaulting? Those poles are twenty feet long, and there isn't a ceiling in the building over ten."

"Give me time, Hack. I'll work it out. Anyway, I think we can get some batons and maybe a couple, three, four teams. We can choose up sides and have a genuine track meet up there after Jerry makes his bed check."

So that's how it began. The First Annual Minnesota Vikings Training Camp Track Meet. It lasted for years.

The next day I stopped in at one of the department stores downtown. Men's colored underwear had just come into fashion, and I picked out matching sets of shirts and shorts in several colors. That afternoon Dale and I loaded up five or six of those eighteen-foot poles on my car's roof and took them back to the dorm. We borrowed some equipment from a maintenance man at the college and cut them down to size. Then we hid the poles in our room.

That evening, while everyone else was either drinking down at Metler's, reading or playing cards in the dorm, or attending a movie, we went out to the track and put several hurdles in the back of my car. Dragging them up to our room through the back stairway took three trips.

When the rest of the guys came in at eleven, they began to harrass us. "Hey, Hunkie. Where were you guys tonight? You got something going on the rest of us should know about?"

"Hackbart, you can tell me about it."

Soon Jerry Burns made his rounds through the second floor. "Alright, girls. It's the bewitching hour. Get in your rooms, or you'll turn into pumpkins."

So we went in our rooms and began to get our things ready. As soon as Jerry was gone, Hack and I began to pass out the uniforms. Yellow for Osborn and Bobby Grimm. Black for Earsell and Charlie West. Red for us.

Our first race was a simple relay. Earsell, Ozzie, and Hackbart had the first lap. Charlie, Bobby, and I ran the final leg. It was pure pandemonium. The dormitory at Mankato is laid out in a rectangular shape, with the rooms on the outside of the hallway and the restrooms and showers on the inside. There was plenty of room to sprint down the straightaway, but the corners resembled roller derby more than a race track.

I stood in front of the guys and gave the countdown. The only problem was I'd forgotten to plan where I would go and was standing ten feet from the nearest door! Down the hallway they came, nostrils flaring, fire in their eyes, legs churning—with me scrambling frantically. When I hit the corner, I kept going right into Milt Sunde and Gary Larsen's room.

After I had recovered, I remembered that I had to run the second lap. I ran down the hallway to get to my spot. I wasn't even turned around and ready when the first three came thundering around the corner and headed right at me.

Hack and I came in last.

The hurdles were next, and the rest of the guys really began hooting when they saw them. We had two sets for the long hallways and one for each end. I don't think any were still standing by the time we had run our two laps. Fighting for position on a running play is tough, but this was murder. Elbows in the ribs. Earsell pulling on my shorts. Bobby tripping us all up. And they had the gall to complain that I was holding on the first corner.

We had just finished maybe the fifth rematch when Bob Hollway came storming through the stairway door. "What the blazes is going on up here?"

"Just a little track meet, Bob."

We were all panting and sweating, and Bob took one look at our matching underwear and began to laugh.

"Track meet!" He shook his head in disbelief. "What's that stuff you're wearing? Fruit of the Loom?"

"That isn't funny, Bob."

"Well, Kassulke, I'll tell you what isn't funny. I've been running the soup out of you guys for two weeks now, but if you don't get enough of it out on the practice field, we'll see what we can do about it tomorrow."

As soon as Bob was safely downstairs, we brought out the poles.

"Announcing the world champion NFL professional pole vaulting king. Dale 'Clothesline' Hackbart!"

"Boo!"

"Whatcha gonna do?" It was Brownie. "Vault yourself through the ceiling?"

"No, out the window!" Marshall.

This time there were more cheers and whistles.

I gave the signal to start, and the Hacker came running down the hall, pole poised, prancing like a drum major.

Gary Larson and Milt Sunde's room was directly off the end of the hall. Their door was wide open and they were lying in their beds taking in the whole show.

Thump. Thump. Thump. Thump.

"Geronimo!"

Hackbart went flying into their room, planted the pole against the bed, vaulted into the air, crashed against the wall above Milt's bed, and landed beside him.

"Hiya, Milt. Nice day isn't it!"

"It's a record, folks. It's a record. The Hacker has done it again. Now he's going to try for a new one."

This time we had him put on Carl Eller's shoes, at least a size fourteen. And we made him put on his Red Baron hat and scarf. By this time the hallway was filled, with barely enough room for him to run down the middle. He ran a gauntlet of pillows in the face, squirts of pop and beer, and the most awful jeering and cheering. It must have distracted him, because he never saw Gary Larson get off his bed and run to his door.

Just as Dale got there, Gary slammed the door.

Wham!

Everybody was laughing and cheering him, until we saw that he wasn't getting up very fast. It turned out that he'd twisted his back and was pretty sore for a couple of days.

If coach Hollway thought that he could wear us out by running us for an extra twenty or thirty minutes a day, I'm sure he was disappointed. The track meet went on again the next night. And from that day on, whenever the dormitory became a little too sedate at night, we'd get out the underwear and walk into the hall.

"OK, you guys. It's time for the track meet!"

It always was.

CHAPTER 17

Le Mans

●

"Punctuality is next to godliness" could have been Bud Grant's motto.

One of his rules was that we were not to be late for anything, and he had his own way of enforcing it. I think he disliked fines as much as he did fights on the field, so he found more subtle ways of informing a person that he was disappointed in his behavior. Often it was just that ice-cold, grey-eyed stare. Occasionally, it would be a public reminder that a particular standard was expected, and this or that person had failed to meet it.

During training camp Bud would always have us leave Mankato for Metropolitan Stadium in Bloomington as late as possible. Even when we were playing in town, he never wanted us around the stadium much more than an hour before the game. He said that he didn't want us in town messing around and getting into trouble. So for Saturday evening games, which most exhibitions games are, he made his announcement about the time we could leave training camp sometime on Friday evening or at breakfast on Saturday.

"Gentlemen," he would say. "Everybody who has a car here can drive from Mankato to the stadium. The rest of you will ride the bus. Now, the game is at 8:00, so the bus will not leave until 5:02."

That was his way of getting our attention.

"5:02?" we would say. "Why then?"

"That's the time we will leave."

"But why?"

And he would answer, "The bus leaves at 5:02, and nobody

will leave early. At that time I will get on the bus, and we will all leave together."

The first Saturday this rule was in force everybody was sitting around, either in their cars or on the bus. We were gunning our motors and threatening one another with all sorts of mayhem.

"Hack, what do you think of all this 5:02 business?"

"Gee, I don't know, Hunkie. I guess he doesn't want us to leave till 5:02."

So we waited another five minutes.

Bud was standing by the door of the bus. Every few minutes he'd glance at his watch.

"You know something, Hack? This is crazy. We're all sitting around here gunning our motors and wasting all this gas. It's 5:00, and I'm going."

Jim Marshall must have been thinking the same thing, because he backed out of his parking space and zoomed down the street. So did Warwick and a few others.

The bus left at 5:02.

After the game, Bud came into the locker room. One of the first things he said was, "There were several players who left early today, and those players will have to be disciplined. I told you that the bus leaves at 5:02, and I don't want anybody leaving before then."

We got the message.

On our way back to Mankato, the Hacker and I talked about what had happened. By the time we got back we had hatched our plan, and that night we explained it to the rest of the team.

On the next Saturday that we were to play in Bloomington, we all got out to the parking lot early and got our cars lined up in a row. It was never done any prettier at Le Mans.

When Bud came out to the bus at about a quarter to five, there we all were, standing by our cars and at attention.

He never batted an eyelash.

At ten minutes to five I walked up to the front of the line and shouted, "Gentlemen, start your engines."

There we were, maybe ten or twelve men roaring and gunning our cars, with Bud standing by the bus with that subtle smile in his eyes. I was standing out in front of the first car holding my red bandana by my side.

It turned 5:02.

Bud turned, stepped into the bus, and the door closed.

I whipped my arm into the air. My bandana went flying.

Marshall nearly ran over me. That was the one possibility for which I had not planned.

As soon as I recovered my bandana, I ran to my car and jumped in. We were off in a cloud of smoke and screeching rubber. It turned into a race to see who would get to the stadium first. Mankato's streets were suddenly filled with Vikings driving like madmen to see who could get out of town the fastest.

Bud never said a word.

The only negative note came when the citizens of Mankato called the police department to complain about the group of crazies driving through town like maniacs. The chief of police came out to the training camp to talk with Bud the next week, and afterwards Bud told us to slow down while driving through town. Today such speeding seems not only wrong, but stupid. At that time in my life, though, I was still living under the illusion that I was exempt from any of life's tragedies. Since such things could never happen to me, I never thought about the possibility of hurting anybody else either.

Before the next home game, Jim Marshall talked to Bud about letting him start the exodus that week, and Bud agreed. So, come a quarter to five on Saturday afternoon, the cars were all lined up in a perfect row. I had gotten out there about noon, and my car was in the pole position. Marshall was out there with a starter's gun and one of those big white flags they use for auto races.

Bud had announced that we all would start by Jim's clock, since he was the team captain and had talked with him about it. Jim would be the official timekeeper; and at the appointed

My brother Willard (*L)* and I.

My mother and grandfather
(William Kassulke) with me.

The Kassulke clan:
(*Bottom, L to R*)
Kathy, Chris, and
Carmen. (*Top, R to L*)
Dad, Willard, Mom,
and me.

September 29, 1962.
Touchdown. My first of
two for Drake that day.

If looking fierce could
win ball games . . . .
(Photo: *Des Moines
Register and Tribune*)

Coach Van Brocklin with his class. (Photo: Skip Heine)

If smiles and songs could win games, John Campbell and Tommy Mason would have done it. (Photo: Skip Heine)

Reading to Kory (*L*) and Kurt (*R*). We all enjoyed this nightly ritual.

In Hawaii for the NFL Players Association Convention. (*L* to *R*) Grady and Nancy Alderman, Elaine and Fran Tarkenton, me and Jan.

It was a joy to serve as the campaign director for the Greater St. Paul Chapter of the March of Dimes for seven years, as well as state chairman for one year. Above, with Arnold Palmer, the national chairman that year.

At the March of Dimes Snowmobile Marathon in St. Paul.

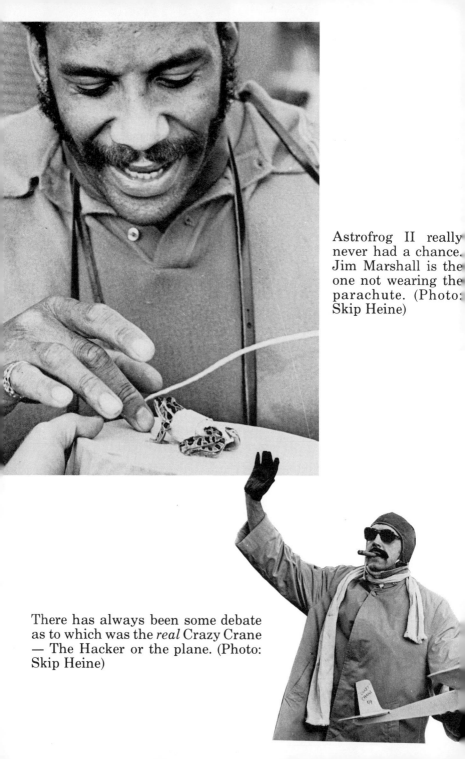

Astrofrog II really never had a chance. Jim Marshall is the one not wearing the parachute. (Photo: Skip Heine)

There has always been some debate as to which was the *real* Crazy Crane — The Hacker or the plane. (Photo: Skip Heine)

Above, training camp was a time for both drills and contact. Below, it also contained its share of relaxed conversation with good friends (*L to R*) Wally Hilgenberg, Lonnie Warwick, and Roy Winston. (Photo: Skip Heine)

Above, it was always a pleasure to separate the runner from the ball with a good tackle. Below, playing on the special teams gave me many opportunities to block field goal attempts. (Photos: Skip Heine)

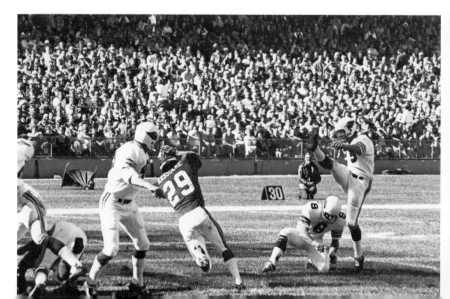

Learning to stand at orderly attention during the playing of the national anthem was part of Bud Grant's schooling in self-discipline. (Photo: Skip Heine)

Consulting with "the doctor of quarterbacks" on the sideline. (Photo: Skip Heine)

Now *you* tell me. Is that a face, or is that a face! (Photo: Skip Heine)

"I never had to chase a quarterback a hundred yards" — Carl Eller. (Photo: Skip Heine)

Yes, he does smile! (Photo: Skip Heine)

When Fran Scrambled, we never knew whether to laugh . . .

or hide! (Photos: Skip Heine)

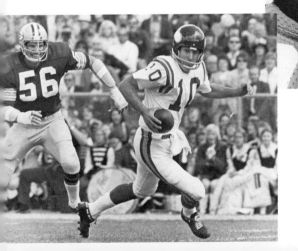

We had a knack for coming up with the big play on the defensive team. Above, Jim Marshall scores on a fumble recovery. (Photo: Skip Heine) Below, I am taking delight in purloining one from Mike Ditka of the Bears. (Photo: *Chicago Tribune*)

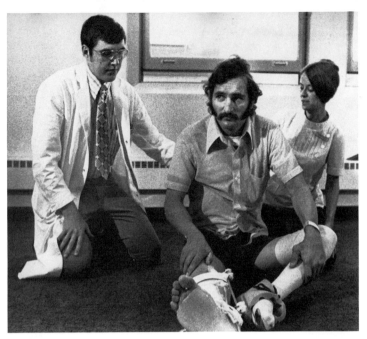

Dr. Tom Szymke and Jeanne Kogl helped me to adjust to using the back brace. It helped me sit erect without further damage to my Spine. (Photo: *The Milwaukee Journal*)

"Ironsides," the van Paul Mergens and I used for traveling to appearances. (Photo: Office of University Relations, Drake University)

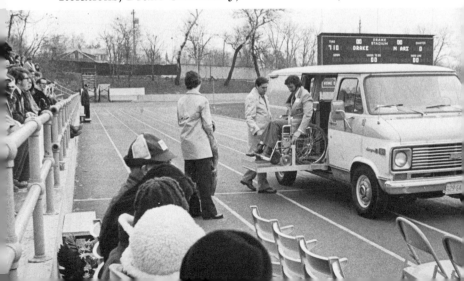

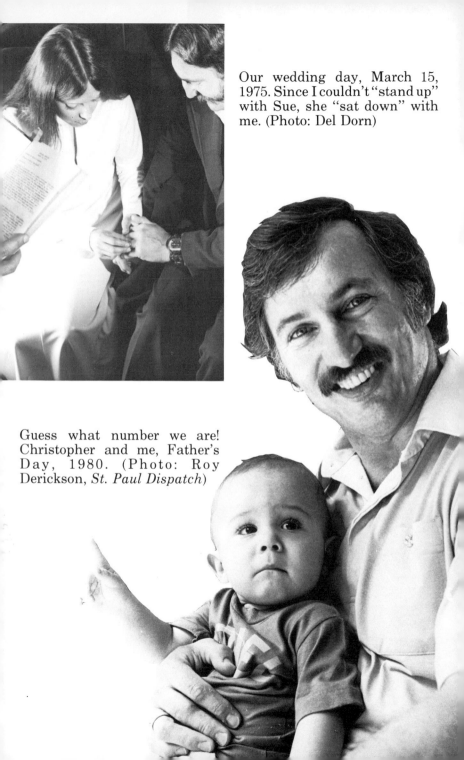

Our wedding day, March 15, 1975. Since I couldn't "stand up" with Sue, she "sat down" with me. (Photo: Del Dorn)

Guess what number we are! Christopher and me, Father's Day, 1980. (Photo: Roy Derickson, *St. Paul Dispatch*)

Nobody can smile like my mother! (Photo: Office of University Relations, Drake University)

"Grand Fiddler" at the benefit concert for the St. Paul Chamber Orchestra. Perfect form!

The Minnesota Vikings basketball team: (*Top, L to R*) Chuck Foreman, Ed White, Matt Blair, Doug Sutherland, Stu Voight. (*Bottom, L to R*) Bobby Bryant, yours truly, Ahmad Rashad. (Photo: Bobby Bryant, Sports Promotions, Inc.)

On the field again, this time as a coach at Bethel College in St. Paul. (Photo: Paul Gavic)

My family: (clockwise from top) Kurt, Kory, me, Christopher, Sue. (Photo: Neil Kveberg)

time he would nod to Bud, Bud would get on the bus, and Jim would fire his starter's pistol.

When Hack and I heard what was scheduled, we dug around in our lockers and came up with a couple of M-80 firecrackers. The big ones!

"Gentlemen, to your cars."

It was ten to five.

"Gentlemen, start your engines."

Two minutes to five.

There were about fifty seconds left when the Hacker lit one of the M-80's, leaned out the door, and threw it under my car. It rolled over under Carl Eller's.

Kaboom!

The guys down at the end of the line floored their foot pedals, and their cars came roaring out of line. Jim gave a desperate look at his watch, shrugged his shoulders, and threw the flag. One by one we peeled out of line and went chasing out of town. Only this time we at least tried to keep our speed under control.

After the game Bud walked up to Marshall, who still hadn't figured out how it had gone wrong.

"Jim. You started the guys too early."

"But coach, they took off before I threw the flag."

"Well, if you hadn't fired that darn gun they wouldn't have done it."

"But Bud, I didn't fire the gun."

Bud just looked at him sadly. It was as if he were thinking, *Don't tell me the crazy bug has bitten him, too.* And then he answered.

"Well, I guess we're just not disciplined enough to do this kind of thing right."

CHAPTER 18

Like a Three-Ring Zoo

●

There was always something happening in the dormitory. One night I awakened, my bed soaked, disoriented. It had to be 2:00 in the morning.

"Aw, no!" I muttered. "A grown man wetting his bed. What am I ever going to say about this?"

Suddenly the Hacker came tearing into the room.

"Hunkie. I think it was Warwick and Winston. Maybe John Kirby, too."

"What?"

"Winston and Warwick just doused us with pails of warm water."

"Oh, great!"

"Great? Whaddaya mean, great?"

"Well, I thought it might have been something else."

"Maybe it was in your case, Hunkie."

"Aw, come on, Hack."

"Look, I saw their shadows by your bed. I'm sure it was Winston, and if he was in on it Warwick was, too. I chased 'em down the hall, but it was dark and they got away. I think they're in Kirby's room."

Well, nobody in his right mind would tangle with Lonnie Warwick. Especially at 2:00 in the morning in a dark hallway. So we cleaned up the beds, found some extra blankets in the dresser, and went back to sleep.

By the next morning the Hacker had already planned our revenge. All that day we ignored the subject of the wet beds. Lonnie dropped a couple of hints, but we let them pass unnoticed.

That night we came back from Metler's early. Warwick and Winston were still out. During the day we had stopped to see a friend of Hack's at the police station and had talked him into letting us use his can of Mace that evening.

We maced both side of their pillows.

It must have been awful stuff, because the next morning when Winston and Warwick woke up their eyes were swollen nearly shut, and Bud had to send them to an eye specialist. When they got back the Hacker was waiting for them.

"You know, you guys really shouldn't be drinking so much."

"Aw, come on, Hack. You know we only had a few beers last night."

"I know. But they say that the stuff kind of accumulates in you as you get older. You can be drinking along as happy as anything, and then one day. . . . Wham! It hits you. They say it affects the eyes first."

"Get outa here!"

They went lumbering up the stairs like a couple of blind buffaloes.

Normally, it was Jerry Burns who checked the rooms at night. Nobody wanted to do it, since it was next to impossible to get everyone on the veterans' floor quieted down and sleeping. Before one end of the dorm could be quieted, something would explode at the other end. We enjoyed fooling with Jerry, and he wasn't above messing with us on occasion, either.

One night Hack and I were in our room—for a change, early, about 11:15. We were in the middle of one of those great Hackbart stories when Jerry poked his head in the door and asked, "Where are Winston and Warwick?"

We both knew where they were: Metler's.

Warwick had been drinking and was a bit under the weather. He had a tendency to become belligerent when he was in that condition and had persuaded Roy that they just weren't going to come in that night.

"The 'ell with Jerry Burns," he said. "The 'ell with 'em all!"

Never mind that we were acting like junior high schoolers

on their first overnight trip, but we agreed to try to cover for them. So when Jerry asked us where they were, I said, "Oh, I don't know, Jerry. The were here less than . . . oh, three minutes ago. Maybe they're in the head."

So off Jerry went. Five minutes later he was back.

"They weren't in the can, Kassulke."

"Yeah? Well, Dickson just left here and said he'd seen them down in Grady Alderman's room."

Five minutes later he was back. Alderman had sent him to Eller's room, and Eller had sent him back to ours.

"Doggone it, Karl. I've been all over the place. They're just not here, and I'm putting them on report."

"You can't do that, Jerry. I was just in the can, and both of 'em walked through laughing at the story Marshall had told them."

We chased Jerry around the floor like this for another twenty minutes.

"I heard them say they wanted to talk with Bud about a problem."

"I heard Roy say they were going upstairs."

"They walked past my room just a minute ago."

By this time Jerry was getting ripe.

In the meantime, Eller, Dickson, and Marshall had sneaked out of the dorm, borrowed somebody's old pickup truck, and drove down to Metler's. They got both Winston and Warwick out of there and threw them into the back. When they got back to the dorm, they helped them upstairs and put them into their beds.

"Kassulke. I've had enough of this," Jerry was saying. "You've gone too far this time. You and Hackbart are going on report along with Winston and Warwick."

Marshall was standing in the hall right behind him. He signalled that everything was safe.

"Jerry, I don't understand what's come over you tonight, but I swear I was just down there to see what the problem was, and they were both in their beds sleeping like babies. C'mon. Let's go down there, and I'll show ya."

He looked at me like I was crazy, but went along.

"See, Jerry. Don't they look sweet when they're sleeping?"

"I don't know how you did it, Kassulke, but I'm going to get to the bottom of this!"

He went stalking down the hall, this time really angry.

Once he was safely off the floor, we all ended up in Grady Alderman and Mick Tinglehoff's room. Grady and Mick had a little refrigerator in their room and kept pop and beer in it. We had a little celebration about pulling one over on Jerry. Soon we had forgotten why we were there and had begun our usual revelry.

We must have been making too much noise, because suddenly somebody poked his head in the door and yelled, "Hey, guys, Jerry just went into Hunkie's room!"

He always checked our room first. He must have thought that if we were in bed the dormitory would be quiet.

We tried to get out the door, but he was already checking rooms halfway down the hall. There was no way to get out. Tinglehoff and Alderman jumped into their beds. John Kirby jumped under Mick's bed. Paul Krause hid in the closet, and Hackbart hid behind the door.

There was no place left for me!

Then I saw the sink. It was placed just around the corner, facing the closet, and couldn't be seen from the door. So I jumped up on it and held onto the light fixture for dear life.

Slam!

Jerry threw open the door. It hit Hackbart in the face.

"Tinglehoff, you and Alderman . . ."

He looked under the beds. He grabbed Kirby.

". . . and Kirby, you . . ."

He turned and saw Hackbart and Krause.

". . . and Hackbart and Krause. You're all fined $250."

And he walked out.

I was still standing on the sink in my undershorts, hanging on to that hot light. And he never even looked at me!

The next day Bud called all five of them, plus Winston and Warwick, over after practice. I went along and stood there laughing while Bud told them how they were setting a bad example for the rookies and were wasting their energy and so forth. He then fined them.

Warwick was furious.

"Hey, what about Kassulke?"

"What about him?"

"He wasn't in his room, either."

"Oh, come on, Lonnie. Tattling isn't becoming to a man of your stature."

I solemnly agreed.

Lonnie must have complained about it for a week. Finally, Hackbart cleared the air. "What're you crying about, Lonnie? You'd have been in real trouble if Jerry had caught you out of the dorm."

I was just grateful to whoever had done such a good job of installing that sink and light.

Jerry Burns was deathly afraid of snakes—all reptiles and bugs, for that matter. That was the source of more than one good prank.

During the game films it was common for someone to drop a stage spider rigged to a fishing line down from the ceiling into the projector's beam. We also bought stage props of snakes and left them in places where he couldn't miss them during his room inspections.

One season we had a real problem in the dorms over this issue because Clint Jones actually loved snakes. In fact, one year he even brought along a little glass aquarium for the grass snakes he found while we were practicing. He fed them frogs and insects, and they were generally well-accepted on our floor.

Not by Jerry.

"Why do you want a snake for a pet, Clint? What good is it? Does it bark or roll over? Will it lick your hand? Can it play dead? Or purr?"

Clint would just smile.

One day one of his snakes got loose.

The maids changed our linens and cleaned our rooms every afternoon while we were practicing. That day, as one of the older ladies came into Clint's room to strip his bed, she noticed the snake sunning itself on the bedspread. She thought it was one of those rubber snakes you can buy in a dime store, so she reached down to pick it up.

It slithered to the floor. She fainted.

She must have hit her head when she fell, because she was taken to the hospital in an ambulance.

That night Bud talked to us before the film session started. "Men, the maids have decided that they won't clean second floor until all the reptiles are gone. So if you want your rooms cleaned, you will have to get rid of them all."

We never did find that missing snake, though.

CHAPTER 19

Teach a Rookie to Drink

●

Sometimes it was difficult, even during training camp, to separate football from the rest of life.

We had been in training camp about a week when one of the ball boys came up to me.

"Mr. Kassulke. There's somebody on the phone who says he just has to talk to you right away."

"Did he say who he was?"

"No, he wouldn't say."

I couldn't figure out who would want to talk to me so badly, so I took off for the phone.

"This is Karl Kassulke."

"Yes, Karl. Jeno's Pizza. Duluth."

Oh, no!

"Karl, we're getting kind of low on those bags. Do you know when the new ones are scheduled to come in? I thought they'd be here by now."

"Well . . . Yeah. I would have thought so, too."

"Could you check on them for me?"

"I'd be glad to. Just give me a few minutes. I put in the order. I know I did. Something must have happened."

I hung up.

The Hacker was standing not ten feet away.

"Hunkie! What's the matter? You look awful. Is it anything serious?"

"Is it anything serious! Just before I came down here I took a huge order for Jeno's Pizza in Duluth, and I forgot to call it in to Cellu-Craft."

"That's serious, Hunkie."

"Hack, if he finds out that I forgot to put in the order, he's going to cancel it. I just know it. And I'll lose all that beautiful commission."

"*That* is something to worry about!"

So we began to talk. There had to be a delay, and it had to be believable. And I didn't want it to be too near the truth.

"I've got it, Hack! I've got the perfect answer."

Within minutes I was in the middle of my explanation.

"I talked with the home office in Chicago, and they told me what happened. The order went in, all right. And everything was done just the way you asked for it. But the truck was hijacked yesterday just as it left the plant."

"Hijacked?"

"Yeah, hijacked. Anyway, we're going to put the whole thing through again, and you should get your bags within a week or so."

"They said it was hijacked? A truck load of pizza bags?"

"Yeah, it does sound crazy, doesn't it? But that's what happened."

And he believed me.

Jeno's Pizza got their bags in due time.

And me? The commission check came through right on time.

Some of us veterans took it upon ourselves to initiate the rookies drafted for the positions we were playing. It wasn't that we picked on them. Actually, we always figured that the better each of our back-up men understood the game, the better it would be for the whole team.

But we did tend to overdo it on occasion.

When Jeff Wright joined the team in 1971, it soon became obvious that he had what it would take to make the team. He was fast and strong. And smart.

We were soon to learn just how smart he was.

One evening Bobby Bryant, Hack, and I decided that since Jeff had so much ability, we really ought to instruct him in some of the finer points of playing in the defensive backfield.

We hustled him off to Metler's bar at 4:30 the next afternoon and proceeded to teach the rookie how to drink. At 5:55 we all went tearing out the back door, running down the alley to my car, and zipped up the hill. As usual we walked in the dining room when the clock turned 6:00.

We ate from 6:00 to 6:15 .

The team meeting wasn't until 7:30, so back we went to Metler's. We began drinking in earnest. Harvey Wallbangers. Teaching Jeff Wright how to drink.

What we didn't notice was that Jeff was stashing much of his in the potted plants by the tables. The rest of us chugged Harvey Wallbangers for over an hour.

By the time we got to the auditorium for the latest Chicago Bears flick, we were in no condition to be doing what we were supposed to be doing.

Bobby sat near the back door of the auditorium.

"I know I'm going to be sick," he groaned.

Jeff smiled and wandered off to the opposite side of the auditorium.

The Hacker and I shuffled down behind Neil Armstrong and several other coaches.

I began to feel uneasy.

"Hack, I think I overdid it."

He just sat there and giggled.

The film began to roll. At first I could roughly follow the movement of the plays, but soon I was getting groggy and my stomach queasy. *Well*, I thought to myself, *it's going to be a long night*.

It didn't turn out to be that long.

The next thing I knew my stomach was boiling. I tried to get up quickly, but ended up half falling against the Hacker.

I tried again.

Then it was too late. Upchuck!

"What the blazes is happening?"

It was Neil Armstrong. He had been directly in front of me.

In panic, I jumped over the seats, tore up the aisle, out the door, and down the hall to the bathroom.

When I got back to the auditorium, I could see that Bobby wasn't in any better shape than I had been. Hackbart was only slightly better. And across the auditorium, smiling brightly, was that slick rookie.

Then the joking began, with Marshall leading the way.

"Sure, Kassulke. Teach a rookie to drink."

I never lived it down.

During the rest of that training camp Jeff would ask me when I was ready to give him lesson number two.

After the meeting Bud motioned for Hack and me to come over and talk. "Karl, maybe you need to learn to drink in moderation, rather than taking these rookies out."

That's all he said.

Well, almost.

He must have spoken to someone else because my next paycheck was a little short.

Many of our shenanigans, like the choo-choo train, grew out of our Wednesday evening escapades at Metler's.

We'd been laughing about the incident with Jeff Wright. After a couple of beers Bill Brown really got on our case.

"You guys have to stop messing with these rookies. You're messing these youngsters' minds up. And you're not helping yourselves, either."

We all laughed, because we knew that Brownie, a subtle practical joker, was really imitating Bud.

"Aw, go blow your whistle!"

"You're just jealous, Hackbart. I bet you had never even seen a whistle like this before I showed it to you."

Brownie's whistle was unique. When he blew it, a person would swear that there was a train in the next room. Brown was an enthusiastic train buff and even had an authentic conductor's hat. He hung both his hat and his whistle in his room as decorations.

As we drove back to the dorm, we developed our newest idea. The choo-choo train.

When we got there, I went into Brownie's room and borrowed his cap and whistle.

We had picked up a big jug of Mogen David red wine a few days earlier, and we dug it out of Hack's closet and opened it. I put the conductor's cap on my head, and we began to march around the hallway.

Choo-choo-choo-choo.

It didn't look much like a train, but it sure sounded like one.

We began pounding on doors as we passed down the hall.

"C'mon out!" Hack was laughing. "We're going to have a little chugging contest with our train."

I kept blowing the whistle.

Before long we had Marshall, Page, Eller, Warwick, Winston, and maybe a half dozen others. We were all following one another down the hall, hands on the hips of the guy ahead of us.

Everyone was chanting, "Chug. Chug. Chug. Chug. Choo. Choo. Choo. Choo."

I was leading the train, Brownie's blue and white conductor's hat perched on my head, and blowing that crazy whistle. The guys kept passing that bottle of Mogen David from player to player.

Soon Jack Patera, the defensive line coach, came through the door. "Alright! I've had enough of this noise. Put the whistle away and take the train hat off! And knock off the train nonsense."

He finally got us all quiet and in our rooms.

I lay there in my bed thinking about that silly whistle. The more I thought about it, though, the more I began to laugh inside. Finally, I crawled out of my bed, sneaked back into Brownie's room, and borrowed his whistle and cap.

I began marching around the dorm again.

Soon we all were at it.

Choo, choo, chug, chug.

Finally we stopped and sat on the floor outside my room drinking wine, blowing the whistle, and telling stories. I don't know why we didn't see him, but suddenly Jack was there.

"Give me that whistle!" He grabbed it out of the Hacker's hands.

Hack jumped up and yelled, "Get your own whistle boy," but when he turned around he looked as shocked as Patera.

"Sorry, coach. Didn't recognize the voice."

That ended it, at least for that night.

But just like the track meet, the choo-choo train became one of our traditions. When things got a little too quiet, someone would go into Brownie's room, grab the whistle and cap, and come out in the hall.

"Alright, you guys. All aboard."

CHAPTER 20

Astrofrog and Thumper

●

Every training camp had its own flavor, and in 1969 our camp centered around rockets.

Training camp is a unique institution in our society—one of the last places where a small group of men exercises almost total authority over the lives of others. Therefore, the players' efforts to express their individuality often take on unusual dimensions.

Like the rockets.

One afternoon, Fred Cox came back to the dorm carrying a large, neatly wrapped package.

"Hey, Freddie. You trying to smuggle something in here?"

"Naw, it's just something I picked up at the hobby shop downtown."

Several of us crowded into his room while he unwrapped his package.

"A rocket?"

"Freddie, what're you going to do with that thing?"

"You'll see."

Well, we did see. Over the next few days he put it together, and one day he and the Hacker went out to the practice field to launch it. Hack was ecstatic when he came back to the room.

"Hunkie, I've just got to get me one of those rockets."

The next day we both went downtown to the toy store. We looked at several rockets, but Hack became even more interested in the model airplanes. He bought himself a classic model and proceeded to assemble it.

Hack had picked up the nickname "the Crazy Crane," so that is what we christened his airplane. On the day appointed for its maiden voyage, he dressed up in his Red Baron cos-

126

tume of baggy pants, beret, scarf, and flying goggles. When we got to the field, half the team was waiting for us, along with a couple of reporters and photographers from the local press. Hack made a speech for the occasion that would have warmed the heart of any politician, and then all attention tuned to the plane.

It took off beautifully. As a matter of fact, it ran very well. Too well.

Hack had put too much fuel in the tank, and it wouldn't stop running. It was one of those planes that would only come down once the fuel was gone.

Hack was desperate. It had to be ninety degrees in the shade, and he was running around that field with all those hot clothes on, his scarf flowing out behind him. Finally, he could take it no longer and began to strip off some of the heaviest clothing.

In the meantime, the plane kept going—in a straight line.

As it moved beyond the range of the radio control box, Hack lost control over it. It headed right on out over the football fields. By the time it ran out of gas, it was over a farmer's cornfield almost a mile away.

We thought we knew where it had landed, but by the time we walked for a mile and began our search, we weren't so sure. We walked up and down the rows of corn arguing with and yelling at each other for an hour or more.

"Hack, don't you think it went further than this?"

"No, Hunkie, I'm sure this is the place."

Twenty minutes later. "Hack, I really think we should walk a little further."

"Hunkie, I'm getting real aggravated by your nagging. We will find it right here if we have to walk all day."

We did eventually find it, and the Crazy Crane was in good condition.

Both of us had been wrong. We had walked too far before starting to look!

After Fred's rocket and Hack's Crazy Crane, several other players decided to get in on the show. Four of them, Jim

Marshall, Ed White, Mick Tinglehoff, and Milt Sunde, decided to build a rocket together. They went downtown and came back with a monstrosity over four feet tall. They weren't content, though, just to have the largest rocket in camp.

They also wanted a passenger!

Since it was obvious that, football players or not, none of us was stupid enough to volunteer, they found a frog which they christened "Astrofrog."

There was room for Astrofrog in the nose cone of the rocket. The idea was that the twin rockets on the sides of the missile would carry the rocket up into the sky and, once the fuel ran out, the heavy nose cone would tip downward and fall off the empty tank. This would free Astrofrog, who would then gently float back to earth with his parachute.

What actually happened was quite different.

The rocket was large enough that they had to use Jim Marshall's car to get it started. But when it fired, only one of the rockets engaged. Instead of going straight up into the air and turning over gently, thus dropping out Astrofrog, it went up at an angle. To make matters worse, they had wired it wrong, and the second rocket kicked in as the rocket began its descent. It blasted straight into the ground!

Astrofrog never had a chance.

They made other attempts to launch a frog, but none of them worked, either. In the end they finally gave up.

Even the philosopher got bitten by the rocket bug.

Paul Dickson was a perfect illustration of the Dr. Jekyl and Mr. Hyde syndrome that seems to be part of the character of so many football players. A ferocious, almost violent man on the field, he was gentle and rather quiet off it.

He spent days assembling his rocket, painting everything just so and putting on the letters and markings perfectly. It was by far the most beautiful rocket in camp, and he absolutely refused to shoot it off.

One Wednesday evening the Hacker and I were in our room. It must have been about 11:30, and we were in the middle of one of the arguments we had begun at Metler's when this awful racket commenced in the hall.

Dickson had spent his free evening reading, as usual. He was in the middle of a good book when Lonnie Warwick walked into his room, looked at him, and grabbed his rocket.

As he ran down the hall you could hear Lonnie sing, "I've got Dickson's rocket! I've got Dickson's rocket!"

This was too much for Paul, and he came out of his chair with a roar and went charging out into the hallway yelling and hollering. "Warwick. You give me that rocket back, or I'll kill ya!"

Lonnie ran into his room, slammed the door, and started his chant all over again.

"I've got Dickson's rocket!"

Paul began to pound on the door, hollering and screaming at Warwick that he'd kill, mutilate, cripple, and do just about everything else to him when he caught him. Finally he gave up.

All the way back up the hall he was muttering and cursing to himself, but before long he was quietly reading his book again.

About ten minutes later, Lonnie's door opened. Smiling, he sneaked down the hallway to Dickson's room, jumped in the doorway, and began yelling, "I've got Dickson's rocket!" He continued his chant all the way back to his room.

Now, nobody messed with Dickson like that. Not even Warwick. In the first place, he was seldom seen without an awful scowl on his face, and anyone who looks that irritated just shouldn't be bothered. He also kept a .38 caliber revolver in his desk.

He came out of his room in a rage. "Warwick—when I get my hands on you I'm gonna kill ya! I'm going to shoot you. That's what I'm going to do. I'll shoot you, and then I'm going to take my hunting knife and cut you up in pieces."

Hack and I looked at each other. This was hilarious, but it could get awfully serious if it went much further.

After another hour of this, we finally went back into our

room. It was late, and we were lying in our beds laughing about those two big guys fighting like that. Then we heard someone walk by our door. It was Dickson.

In spite of their rowdy natures, Warwick and his roommate Winston had a soft streak in their heart. They had found a couple of baby rabbits outside and had brought them up to their room. They had cleaned out a corner of their locker and had fixed up a little box for them with torn newspapers and socks for warmth. And they fed them lettuce and grass because they were sure they couldn't survive outside.

Paul knew this.

There was a very deliberate knocking on Warwick's door.

"Warwick, if that rocket isn't back in my room by tomorrow morning, I will come in there, and I will wring the necks of those two little bunnies in your closet. And that's the last time I'm going to tell ya."

Compassionate, gentle Paul Dickson threatening to dispatch two little rabbits off to happy bunny land!

The next morning the rocket was back sitting on his desk. And I have no idea whether or not he would have done it.

CHAPTER 21

Rhonda's Clock

●

My dad always told me not to mess with an eating dog. "Chances are it'll bite you, Karl," he would say.

He never warned me about Hackbart.

We were always hungry. The coaches understood that, and there was an abundance of food at every meal. They even scheduled snacks when they were appropriate. But that did not solve the problem of nighttime—it's a long time between dinner and breakfast when a person is as active as we were.

We always tried to lessen some of the discomfort at Metler's, but a pitcher of beer just doesn't feel very solid in the stomach. Frequently we would pick up food to take back to the dorm, but that's where the trouble began.

It was nearly impossible to get any food into one's room. Carrying it into the dorm was easy—there weren't any rules against such snacks—but getting it past the rest of the guys was something else.

"Whatcha got, Hunkie?"

"Nothing much. Just a little snack."

"What do you mean, 'a little snack?' That pizza must be two feet wide!"

Heads would pop out of rooms all along the hall. "Did somebody mention pizza?"

"Hey, thanks a lot, Karl. You're a real friend."

By the time I'd get to my room I was lucky if there was one piece left for me.

This went on every year. Both the Hacker and I tried all sorts of tricks to get our food by our teammates. How do you hide a warm pizza? We once discussed holding it high above our heads and pretending that we were really carrying a round jigsaw puzzle. But we knew that wouldn't work. The smell alone would give us away.

So we switched to sandwiches. Hoagie sandwiches. Much easier to hide. Except from each other!

One night I came into our room, and Dale had a big submarine sandwich in both hands. The other half lay on his bed. I watched him for a few seconds. Then I walked over to his bed.

"Hack, can I have the half you've got on the bed?"

"No, Hunkie. I want it all!"

"Look, Hack. I'll order a pizza or something. I'll buy one tomorrow. Just let me have that sandwich. Please!"

"That's right, Hunkie. Lay the guilt trip on me. You've stolen so many of my sandwiches and pizzas, there's no way I'm going to share this one with you. Remember last week when you stopped the delivery boy by the door and took the pizza? Huh? You remember that?"

"But Hack, I was starving."

"Yeah? Well, so was I. But guess who got to eat it! And I had to pay for the thing!"

"Look, Hack. I'll pay you for that sandwich."

"Pay for the pizza instead! Sorry, Hunk. I want the whole thing."

I could see that there was no point in arguing with him, so I sat on my bed. I couldn't stop thinking about how good that sandwich looked, and every time I looked at it I started salivating. Finally I got up, walked back to his bed, and picked up his sandwich. Two bites. That's what I took. Two big bites!

"Give me that!" roared the Hacker.

He grabbed it from my hands and stomped back to his bed. Then he said, "Karl, if you want it so bad, here it is." He threw it on the floor, put his foot on it, and gave it a healthy push.

I didn't mind. I just reached down, dusted it off, and proceeded to eat with great enjoyment.

This infuriated him. He walked over to my side of the room,

unplugged my fan, walked over to the open window, and threw it out. From two floors up.

"How do you like that, Karl?"

Now I was furious. My fan and a hot night! I threw the rest of the sandwich at him and walked over to his dresser. "Aha!"

It was the little yellow alarm clock his daughter Rhonda had given him as a going-away present for training camp. He was nuts about her and talked about her all the time.

"Don't do it, Karl! That clock means a great deal to me. You know Rhonda gave it to me. It has sentimental value!"

"Good!" Out the window it went.

"Kassulke, you're a crazy fool!" he screamed. By then he had jerked my clock radio off my desk and was heading for the window.

I attacked him. We wrestled to the floor, and then John Michaels, one of the coaches, came in the door. He had been watching for a few minutes and felt it was time to stop the action.

"All right boys, let's break it up."

Later that night I went outside and picked up both his alarm clock and my fan. Both were battered pretty badly. As I stood by my bed later trying to fit the pieces of Rhonda's clock together, I heard the Hacker's laughter.

"What's so funny, Hack?"

"You, Hunkie. An hour ago you were ready to kill me over half a submarine sandwich. Now you're standing there like a whipped puppy with that clock."

It seems funny today, but that night all I could think about was wrecking a little girl's clock. For once I really had felt like a dumb Hunkie.

CHAPTER 22

The Rookie Show

●

The Rookie Show began under Van Brocklin.

As he conceived it, it was one of the final stages in the transformation of a rookie into a professional football player.

"You've got to be able to take it," he would yell.

The Rookie Show usually took place near the end of training camp, just before the final cuts. By then there were maybe six to eight rookies left who wouldn't make the team.

Jim Marshall would come over to Hack and me and say, "Hunkie, we've got to get going on the Rookie Show. It's Friday, and on Monday they're going to lop off all those heads, and there won't be anybody left for the show."

When we were in Bemidji, we rented a room in the back of a restaurant. Early in our history we started having a fish fry for this event. Some of us would go out and buy some of the best-tasting fish that northern Minnesota could supply—fillets of northern pike, walleye, bass. Throughout it all we kept pressuring the rookies to drink.

Once the meal was over, it was time for the Cardinal Puff. This was a coordination game, even though some people misunderstood it as a drinking bout. We would get all the rookies around a large table and Jim Marshall and I started it out. The object of the game was to repeat successfully the words and actions of the preceeding player. Chug-a-lugging a bottle of beer was the penalty for failure.

Marshall would take his bottle in hand and say, "With one finger, here's the Cardinal Puff for the first time tonight."

He'd take a sip. Then he'd quickly tap the top, then the bottom of the table, each knee and each shoulder with one finger, stand up, sit down, and put his hands on the table.

I'd repeat it.

Then it was the poor scared rookie's turn.

"Here's one finger . . ."

"Wrong, rookie! Drink!

He'd drink.

This would continue around the table, with everybody messing up. The more they drank, the more uncoordinated they became. And the more uncoordinated they became, the more they had to drink.

It was either drink with the veterans during the Rookie Show or get the tar beat out of you on the practice field. Everyone had his choice.

One of the key elements of the Rookie Show was the skits. We would get together with the rookies before the show started and explain to them how to make fun of the coaches and veterans. The idea was to exaggerate a person's peculiarities to the point of embarrassment. This was the most entertaining part of the Rookie Show, because we got to see ourselves as others saw us.

I think it was probably Bobby Bryant who put him up to it, but one of the rookies did a parody of me and my Dristan bottle one year. It was delightful.

I've always had a problem with my breathing. A nose that has been broken many times hasn't helped matters any, but I'm told it's congenital. As a result of this problem, I've had to use a spray for years to clear my nasal passages.

The problem was particularly bad during training camp, since the hay fever season was at its peak. Since I had to use it so often I always carried a Dristan bottle in my sock. That way I could inhale a little every time it got difficult to breathe.

Though it worked wonders, I took a lot of kidding about it—mostly on the order of why a big, tough football player would always carry a little white Dristan bottle around.

During the skit the rookie portrayed me as a Dristan addict. I couldn't say a word; I couldn't take a step; I couldn't do anything on that stage without dipping into that sock and sniffing the little white bottle.

"Yeah, Hunkie the Dristan junkie!" yelled the Hacker.

That time the joke was on me.

There were some other hilarious portrayals of players, but our most creative efforts were saved for the coaches. Our favorite was the parody of the team meeting, a delightful way to embarrass all the players and the coaches. We improved on it with every Rookie Show, though the basics remained the same each year. Everybody would be given a role to play, either Bud Grant, another coach, or one of the players.

First came the offensive team meetings, which were just as orderly as the real thing—only in the skit players went beyond mere politeness. People were raising their hands to speak or to go to the bathroom. One guy raised his hand for permission to raise his hand. It was zany. They would say "Yes, sir" and "No sir" when spoken to and make absurdly simple comments about their play assignments.

Then came the defensive team meeting. In real life we were an obnoxious crowd, always heckling the coaches, throwing junk at one another, arguing, making uncomplimentary noises. The defensive skits were always priceless, with guys passing gas and Bob Hollway, our coach, hollering for more sphincter control on the defensive line. The other jokes were about on that level.

Each year by the time the skit was over, Bud would be talking to us. He'd say, "You guys really act like that? Is that how my defensive meetings are conducted?" And he'd turn to the coaches. "Don't you have control over your players?" I suspect that he secretly loved it, but after each Rookie Show the coaches made extra efforts to be sure that our meetings were conducted in a more dignified manner.

One of my fondest Rookie Show memories is from 1969.

One of the rookies, an offensive guard I believe, was dressed up to look like Bud. The imitation was so good that even Bud roared with laughter. He talked like Bud. He walked like him. He gestured like him.

And best of all, he coached like him.

He made one change, though; and it was priceless. He dressed himself up as a robot.

Bud is famous for an iceman image. Nothing actually could be further from the truth, but we loved to tease him about it. The rookie kept walking around the stage imitating Bud, but adding some characteristics of a robot. Every time he had an idea for solving a problem he would start chirping, "Beep, beep. Beep, beep," as if he were getting a message from outer space. He mixed in absurd ideas of his own with Bud's favorite rules. It was a masterful job of acting.

"Beep, beep. Beep, beep. We will make Paul Dickson into a wide receiver."

"Beep, beep. Beep, beep. We will practice standing at attention for the national anthem for fifteen minutes every day."

"Beep, beep. Beep, beep. There will be no smoking in the locker rooms."

"Beep, beep. Beep, beep. There will be no more cookies packed in the airplane meals."

"Beep, beep. Beep, beep. There will be no drinking on weekends before games."

All during that year you frequently could hear someone begin to chirp, "Beep, beep. Beep, beep," during practice.

And every time somebody would say, "Hold it. Bud's getting one of his messages."

Bud would just stand there with his arms folded and his eyes twinkling.

CHAPTER 23

Chinese Fire Drill

●

January 11, 1970. Super Bowl IV.

For me it was the pinnacle, the ultimate. The dream every young boy has of being world champion at something.

Ever since I was a youngster, and then as a high school and college player, I wanted to be the best, to excel. To say to the world, "Hey! I'm Karl Kassulke, and I'm somebody!"

Now I was.

We had fought through those lean years, those years when people laughed at us and called the Vikings a bunch of quitters and losers—"hatchet men." But we kept right on playing our way through the crowd from the bottom to the top. We were the best, and we knew it!

We really believed we would win, and we never prepared more diligently for a game.

We didn't know it at the time, but the tone of the whole event—confusion—was set as soon as we arrived in New Orleans. No one knew how that mood developed. Perhaps it was the mix-up in our room reservations when we arrived. Perhaps it was the fact that when our families came down for the game their reservations were also lost, and most of them had to stay out of town. Perhaps it grew out of the difficulty we had in analyzing the Kansas City Chiefs' offensive and defensive style of play.

It would be easy, especially after reading the earlier portions of this book, to suggest that the Vikings didn't take their football seriously enough, or that we were too busy partying to play football. This wasn't true. Every player on our team, myself included, kept their off-the-field shenanigans out of their football game. We played with a vengeance and intensity. Always.

138

Every player and coach on the team prepared for the Super Bowl game more thoroughly than for any other game that year. Still, something was missing.

Usually a defensive player plays by instinct and reaction. By the time one plays high school, college, and NFL ball, there isn't much an offensive team can throw at a defensive player that he hasn't already seen. For this reason, the game becomes one of observing the way the play develops, remembering what tends to happen when a play unfolds that way, and then executing.

It was different against Kansas City. Hank Stram called it his offense of the seventies. Whatever it was, it confused us. We played with a tentativeness that was out of character.

All week long when we weren't practicing or eating or sleeping, we were in team meetings with linemen, defensive backs, receivers, and so on all having their own. There was none of the usual clowning around—no thrown shoes, no harrassing the coaches, no water balloons. None of that stuff.

We meant business. After all, there was a lot of money at stake, not to mention our pride. We hadn't come this far to blow it by tearing around town drinking and making nuisances out of ourselves. We wanted to win. And we worked to win.

Our defensive backfield meetings revolved around analyzing the Kansas City offense. "What kind of formation is that, Kassulke?"

Bob Hollway had stopped the film, and everyone was looking at me. I'd never seen anything like it, and I tried my best.

"Well, it looks like a . . . strong, right . . . no, a . . . ."

"Winston. What do you think it is?"

"Maybe a . . . no, it looks like a double wing . . . with an inverted tight end."

"Warwick?"

"Coach, I don't know!"

"Now we're getting somewhere! An honest man."

We all laughed. But the uncomfortable truth was that none of us really knew what Kansas City was doing. They moved their players around in such unorthodox formations and variations that it took us days to figure out their system.

We did learn their system. At least, I felt that I had catalogued most of it in my mind. But the problem was that there hadn't been enough time to let it become second nature to me, and time and time again during the game I found myself thinking about the play instead of reacting to it.

On Friday before the game we had to make a decision on how we would defense them. "We'll do this. If they line up on the hash mark, Karl will always go to the strong side of the field . . . unless we blitz. Then Karl will have to stay and take whoever's in the tight end's spot."

This went totally against everything we had always done. More important, it required a totally new way of thinking. Several times I simply out thought myself.

Normally, the strong safety's job is to go to the side where the tight end lines up—"the strong side"—to cover the tight end on passing plays and protect against the run. The rest of the backfield takes their cue from the strong safety before establishing their own positions. Nearly every NFL team uses this system.

In this game, though, I frequently found myself lined up on the wrong end of the line. In getting to my proper position I created quite a stir in the backfield. Defensive backs were jumping all over the secondary.

On one play in particular Hank Stram made a comment indicative of the game when he yelled to his assistant, "Look at Kassulke out there! We've got him so confused he's running around like he's at a Chinese fire drill."

That hurt. Especially since there was so much truth to it.

It didn't help that he knew he was wired for sound for NFL Films. Every year at Super Bowl time, or whenever television shows the highlights of great Super Bowl games, I get the honor of hearing his comments one more time.

There was a time when this made me very angry, but I've come to realize that he really meant nothing personal. And besides, as time passes, I've come to the same conclusion.

I did look like a one-man "Chinese fire drill!"

Even though we were doing what we had planned.

It would be unfair to Kansas City to blame our loss completely on our confusion. Kansas City was a very good team. They had players like Bobby Bell, Buck Buchanan, Willie Lanier, Jan Stenerud, and Lenny Dawson. The oddsmakers had favored us overwhelmingly, some as much as thirteen points. Nobody on the Vikings thought we were thirteen-point favorites, though we did think we would win. After all, as a defense we had allowed the lowest points per game against us in the history of the NFL, and our offense was solid. But we knew Kansas City was good.

In the end it came down to one team grabbing the momentum at the beginning and keeping the other team off balance.

And the big plays. The Vikings have always prospered by the big play, especially that year. The interception that went for a touchdown. The fumble recovery. The quarterback sack. Blocked kicks. These had been our strengths, particularly of the defense. More than one winning effort was enhanced by our giving the ball to the offensive team in excellent field position.

It was different this game.

Early on John Henderson, an excellent wide receiver from Michigan, fumbled the ball after a fine reception. It was his only fumble all year. The next time we got the ball, Charlie West, another sure-handed player, dropped the kick-off on the nineteen yard line. Given the two "end-around" plays that the Chiefs turned into long gainers, three pass interceptions, and several easy passes that we dropped, one can begin to feel the desperation that mounted as the first half progressed. Player after player made key mistakes at crucial moments. The worst of it was that a number of these mistakes were made by men who just never made mistakes.

And then there was mine.

Earsell Mackbee had hurt his shoulder a couple of weeks earlier against Los Angeles when we beat them 23–20 to go to the Super Bowl. His shoulder hadn't totally healed by game time, but he played anyway—and actually played better than most of us. But then he reinjured his shoulder and left the field to get it taped.

It was a crucial series. We had fallen behind 16–0 early in the first half on three Jan Stenerud field goals and Mike Garrett's run of five yards following one of our fumbles. But we had started the second half strong, and Dave Osborn had scored a touchdown about five minutes into the second half.

The momentum had changed. I could feel it. We all could. It was starting to come. And I could see it in the eyes of the Kansas City players. Out of fear, or at least uncertainty, they weren't hitting with the same authority they had shown in the first half. We were doing the intimidating.

Then it happened.

It was a third and long-yardage play from the forty-six yard line. Lenny Dawson tossed a little turn-in to Otis Taylor. Earsell, always the fierce competitor, had reinserted himself into the game as soon as the shoulder was taped and came up to make the tackle. When his shoulder hit Otis's hip, it separated further, and he lost his grip.

Otis was off and running.

If we had been playing our usual defense, I would have had him instead of Earsell. But as it was, I had been covering the deep pattern, since Otis was lined up away from the hash mark. In coming over to make the stop I had a good angle, but as I got to him I was too anxious and moved too quickly. My tackle was low, and when he gave me his move and the stiff arm, I had no leverage that would allow me to hold on to him. He was gone.

Forty-six yards.

I wanted to die right there. I had always prided myself on my sure tackling, and both Bud Grant and Norm Van Brocklin had often used my style as an illustration of how it should be done. I enjoyed the respect that the tight ends showed me, but this time I had blown it. And in the Super Bowl.

It wasn't the mistake that hurt us the most. There were

plenty of mistakes to pass around in that game. But it was *my* mistake, and it happened in a way that everyone watching the game knew who made it. It hurt to let my friends down like that.

When we were in the locker room, Bud summed up the game in typical Bud Grant fashion. "Men, we were beaten by a better team than we were today. Yes, we made mistakes. We made errors we should not have made, and we made errors that we hadn't made all year long. But I'm proud of all of you. I'm grateful to the Almighty for my opportunity to work with such a fine group of men. You're a collection of real winners.

"If we had won today, we would have gone down in sports history as one of the best football teams of all time. But we didn't. We'll have our chance to prove how good we are next year, and for many years to come.

"Men, we will be back . . . because we're winners!"

The Vikings were winners all right.

And, true to Bud's word, we came back.

CHAPTER 24

More Than Football
●

I never saw myself as a taker.

I've always enjoyed giving, whether it was to my family and friends, or to strangers.

Some of my friends have called me an easy mark, but I never saw it that way. It seemed to me that I had received so much more from life than I deserved or needed, and I enjoyed getting out with people and making their lives happier. The result, however, was that I always was on the go.

March of Dimes. Duff's Celebrity Golf Tournament. Speaking at schools and conventions in five states. Coordinating the Vikings basketball team. Operating Sports Celebrities.

I loved it all.

In between football and all these activities, I tried to fit in my family. I was proud of Jan and the boys. Jan had completed her undergraduate studies at the University of Minnesota once we became settled in Minneapolis. Having done extremely well, she enrolled in the medical school at the university. Kurt, our oldest son, and Kory were born two and a half years apart, and I was fiercely proud of both of them. Even as children they were interested in sports, and I took them with me to many of the activities I attended.

With Jan's full-time commitment to her medical studies, I often took on the roles of both mother and father. I could change a mean diaper and was adept at feeding and caring for both boys. I even took a very active part in PTA meetings and other activities with the kids. It wasn't all that easy, but things seemed to be working out reasonably well. Both Jan and I had our own lives, and we were both excelling in our careers.

One of my favorite public commitments was the March of Dimes organization. I have always had a soft spot in my heart for crippled children. It seems so unfair that they have to suffer so much, and the March of Dimes provided me with a way of getting involved as the campaign director for the Greater St. Paul Chapter of the March of Dimes for seven years, starting in 1965.

We used the usual fund-raising efforts. Television. Radio. Business contributions. Some of our activities were more fun, like sponsoring basketball games at Met Center between the Vikings and the Green Bay Packers. We also played basketball games pitting the Vikings' offensive and defensive teams against one another. We supported walk-a-thons, and once I even offered to pay $25 per mile to anyone who could push me on my feet ahead of him that far. I didn't lose much money that day.

Through all these efforts we raised several hundred thousand dollars for the March of Dimes. That money helped fund real progress at the University of Minnesota hospitals in cellular research, birth defect detection systems, and other important areas of research. Those days bring me many warm, fond memories.

Then there was Duff's Celebrity Golf Tournament. I've never been a good golfer. Hackbart still insists that on a good day I was a legitimate forty-five handicapper. Being out there with people was good enough for me, though, and I enjoyed entertaining them even more. My problem was I never seemed to hit the ball straight. It was always either a hook or a slice. The more I tried, the more erratic I became. And my putting was the joke of the tournament.

"I thought the high score won" was my annual joke to help me laugh my way through the day.

The money that was raised each year at Duff's tournament went to the Variety Club Heart Hospital at the University of Minnesota. I always thought that we could have raised as much money if we had just asked people for it, but people seemed to really enjoy the tournament and liked the feeling of involvement. I know I did, and every so often I would drop by the hospital to see what was happening.

After I was injured on the motorcycle, I took the job of introducing the celebrities as they teed off on holes one and ten. It gave me a chance to get back at all those guys who had teased me so unmercifully about my own game.

It did backfire once, though. After the accident Monty Krizan put together a traveling reptile show for school and public appearances all over the country. He has pythons, giant tortoises, Alex the alligator, and even a rhino iguana.

On this particular day I was announcing that Bill Brown was teeing off on number ten when I felt this cool thing crawling down my back. I had noticed that people were backing away from the platform, some even appearing quite frightened, and when I turned in my wheelchair to see what it was, there stood Monty and Hackbart holding Monty's sixteen-foot yellowhead python.

Very few of us thought such a scene as humorous as Monty and the Hacker did! It was just one more of Hack's practical jokes that got him in trouble.

There was another day when he got into trouble without trying to pull a stunt on anybody. I had booked both the Hacker and myself to talk to a civic group in St. Paul. The Hacker had a reputation for being an unnecessarily rough player, and someone from the crowd asked him if he thought that the officials were picking on him by calling so many penalties.

"What do you mean?"

"Do you get penalties called where other players might do the same thing and not get a penalty?"

I was chuckling to myself, because any athlete knows that officials' judgments can be very subjective. I could hardly wait to see how he would get out of this one! He should have received some credit for effort.

"It's like this," he explained. "The officials prepare for games pretty much like players do. They study the game films and learn the characteristics of each player. Things like who holds in the line and how they try to cover it up. Who likes to hit someone when the officials aren't looking. They even spot things that look like penalties, but really aren't."

So far so good.

Then he finished his answer. "Most of the officials keep all this stuff in a little black book, so to speak. They refer to it in preparing for each game. It helps them keep all that information straight and helps them stay alert to what could be happening on the field."

The audience seemed satisfied, and the next question was for me.

"Karl, why do the officials miss so many calls? When they show the plays on instant replay, some of the calls really look awful!"

"Yeah, I know. But I've found out one thing for sure. They're all people out there on the field, not machines. And if you're going to have to depend on a camera to correct the officials' mistakes, what are you going to use to correct the players' errors?"

On our way home we began talking about the evening, especially about these two questions. I told him that I sure hoped he didn't get into any trouble for saying that the officials all carried black books.

His face turned white. "Hunkie, I didn't say that the officials black list players. I just said that they keep track of tendencies. I didn't mean they actually had a black book. Maybe it's green, for all I know. But I know they keep track of us all."

The next morning the St. Paul *Pioneer Press* ran a headline in its sports section that said something like, "HACKBART TALKS ABOUT NFL OFFICIALS' BLACK BOOK."

Poor Hack. He was still at home when Bud called him, and he tried to explain how he had used the term "black book." Bud finally accepted his answer but suggested that he call NFL Commissioner Pete Rozelle before the situation got out of hand.

A few days later this same sports writer was at the stadium watching practice. Hack and I walked over to him. "How could you have done it?" Hack moaned. "I could have been suspended and lost a lot of money."

"Aw, come on, guys. It was just a joke. But didn't it look great in print!"

We had a good laugh together. But we watched what we said in public after that.

Because of my many involvements, I had a tendency to forget some of the commitments I made, both for myself and for others on the team through Sports Celebrities. Hackbart still gives me a rough time about the day I booked him for a punt-pass-and-kick contest in Eau Claire, Wisconsin. And forgot to tell him.

The day came and went, and about nine o'clock that night he received an irate call from the local Ford dealer who had had all those disappointed boys on his hands.

Another time I sent Mick Tingelhoff to speak at a banquet in Sioux Falls, South Dakota. It's about a five-hour drive, and when he got there he found that it had been cancelled.

Still another time I had the Vikings basketball team going to Iowa when they were supposed to be in Duluth.

Why I have these lapses I've never understood, but it's definitely an embarrassing part of my personality.

One of my favorite public appearances as a Viking was at the Fisherman's Day festival in St. Paul. It was there that I established myself as the Vikings' champion in birling, which is the technical word for log-rolling. My agility on my feet going both forward and backward—so necessary for a defensive back—helped me tremendously.

The field had been narrowed to Bill Brown, Hackbart, Paul Dickson, and myself. Paul gave me the biggest scare and was my last competition. He weighed so much more than I did that it seemed like I was a foot and a half out of the water. We must have gone on for nearly a minute before he finally lost his balance.

Winning didn't keep me from getting wet, though. Hack, Paul, and Bill pulled me off that log immediately and proceeded to give me a good dunking.

I was never the most important player on the Vikings. All of us were good players, but the nature of football is such that one player seldom really stands out above the rest. What I enjoyed was the teamwork and the camaraderie, both on and off the field.

Two awards I received were that much sweeter for being unexpected.

In 1967 my teammates awarded me the Terry Dillon Memorial Award, named in honor of a Viking who had died in a construction accident in 1964. The inscription read, "The player who best exemplifies the characteristics of dedication as an athlete and a man." I treasure that honor.

The second award was even more of a surprise.

In 1971 I was elected to play in the Pro-Bowl, an award granted by vote of all the players in the NFL. It's impossible to express how much that award meant to me. Hackbart says I was like a little boy with his first puppy when I heard about it.

We had some great players on the Vikings, and I was always proud to be able to be on the field with them. The truth is, I just wanted to be a part of the team.

Playing in the Pro-Bowl was like icing on the cake. To be chosen by your peers as one of the best! From that day on I walked a little taller and felt like I was one of the most fortunate people ever to live.

I still am.

CHAPTER 25

On the Court

●

It may be difficult to imagine the Vikings playing basketball, but we did.

And with a flair! Or, as some said, with a vengeance.

Earsell Mackbee and I had talked about it long before we actually started the team. The way we looked at it, we could be "roving ambassadors of good will" for the Vikings.

Bud said we could also break our necks!

But we went ahead with the program, and before long we were receiving challenges from as far away as Libby, Montana. The response was surprising. People would pack small gymnasiums and large fieldhouses. We played hard, gave all the entertainment we could, and made it a pleasant evening for everyone.

Earsell was a tremendous basketball player. We called him our "token Globetrotter." He could dribble behind his back and do all sorts of unusual things with the ball. Some of his trick shots I've never seen anybody else do.

The rest of us had our own acts to perform.

Before the game began we'd get together with our opponents and say something like, "Hey, let's have a good time out here tonight. We'll set up some formations and things, and we'll let you get some easy baskets, and everybody will have something to talk about."

Then we would go into our routine. I would usually come over to the bench and pick up the microphone and call the plays. Running plays. Passing plays. Even field goal kicks. One of our favorites was the fake handoff to Bill Brown and a short pass to Charlie West. Charlie was as slick as a cat, and he'd be in high gear before anyone knew what was happening. Whoosh! Down the floor he'd go and slam dunk the ball. This play worked well until the night in North Dakota he hit the rim and shattered a backboard. After we paid for it, Charlie's dunk shots were a little less flamboyant.

Sometimes we'd get booked with a local team that wanted to take the game seriously, and that's usually where trouble would begin. Often these teams were composed of guys who were 6'5" to 6'8," ex-college players who wanted to show their wives and friends—and probably even themselves—that they could hold their own against a bunch of supposedly tough guys like us.

Before long the elbows would start flying, and the pushing would become rougher than normal. We'd have to confront them at a time-out or at halftime. "Hey, guys. Let's stay cool out there. We're here to have a good time, and we don't want anybody to get hurt!"

This approach didn't always work. A game at Sioux Falls was one of those times. We were playing a group of teachers, mostly ex-college athletes. They had enough men to make three or four teams, and there were just seven of us. Having just returned from a road trip of fifteen games, we were tired and easily agitated.

They were playing for blood with fast breaks, a full court press, and lots of substitutions. No way they would go along with gimmick plays, either. They were obviously trying to run us into the ground, and it nearly worked.

Before long a couple of their players began taking cheap shots at our men. We had faced this before, as if these weekend athletes felt compelled to say, "I'm as tough as you Vikings are, and here's to show it!" This time it became dangerous.

On one rebound one of their players clobbered Hackbart on the back of the head. It was totally unnecessary. The Hacker, who nobody ever accused of running away from a challenge, was on him like a cat.

"What are you trying to prove, fella?"

"Cool it, Hack. Cool it. We don't want to give the Vikings a bad image." As usual, Bill Brown's good sense calmed the situation.

With twenty-five hundred people at the game, we really wanted to give them a good show. The only thing to do was to get the game going again.

About five minutes later Bill was going in for a wide open lay-up. He'd broken free on a fast break, but just as he was at the peak of his jump, one of their players ran in and undercut him. Bill hit the floor like a wrecking ball.

Right on his arm and shoulder.

One has to know Bill Brown to appreciate the situation. I've seen him run into the line and get clotheslined or hit after the whistle, and he would bounce back up like a rubber ball and run back to the huddle. "Give it to me again," he'd yell. You couldn't hit him hard enough to make him angry. If you did something unnecessary to him, though, he would take it out on you when he was blocking for someone else. That was just his way.

There was to be no going back into the huddle this time.

Brownie had no more than hit the floor than he was on his feet, chasing this guy all over the floor. Apparently, he thought Bill wouldn't go up into the stands because he ran up into the bleachers. Bill caught him about eight or ten rows above the scorer's table and nailed him on the chin. He dropped like he'd been shot.

By this time both teams' benches had come onto the floor, pushing and shoving one another, and I grabbed the mike.

"That's alright, folks. Everything's going to be OK now. We've got everything under control, and there isn't going to be any fight."

It worked. Everyone calmed down.

We never had those kinds of troubles when Ed White travelled with us. His presence kept games from becoming excessively rough. Ed was probably the strongest man in the NFL. At any rate, he was the NFL arm wrestling champion, and nobody fooled with him or any of his friends. Ed wasn't the world's greatest basketball player, but he sure entertained the crowd.

At halftime he would put on his own show. He'd arm wrestle anybody. I never saw him lose. One night he was feeling particularly feisty and took on two guys at once. He put them both down instantly.

We did get in a little trouble over the incident in Sioux Falls. Of course we weren't totally innocent, but the other player had in a sense asked for his trouble. By the time we got back to Minneapolis, someone had called Jim Finks, Vikings' General Manager, and he called me into his office.

"Hunkie, I know you guys love that basketball thing, and we're not going to stop you from doing it. But, please, if you're going to call yourselves the Vikings basketball team, we can't have any more of these incidents on the floor. It makes the whole team look bad."

I agreed.

And in the future we were more careful about who we let officiate the games.

Not all our troubles came on the floor, though.

We played a group from Mason City, Iowa, one night, and some of their people followed us into the Top Cat Bar at Fort Dodge.

We had played rough. What kind of basketball would people expect from professional football players? But our opponents were still carrying a grudge, and before long they began to get vocal about their feelings toward us.

It didn't help matters at all when someone suggested that one of our unmarried teammates was amorously inclined toward one of their girlfriends. The response to that statement was a fist square on the mouth.

Still, we stayed cool. We were helping the young man to a seat when one of the locals called me a very bad name.

"Sir, that was not a wise thing to say. I'm a very patient man, but you've gone too far. One way or another, you're going out that door."

He chose discretion as the better part of valor, and I

chalked one up to the wisdom of nonviolence.

By this time a rather large crowd had gathered, and some-one who suffered from very poor judgment decided to make an observation about Clint Jones' beautiful ebony skin. Milt Sunde was enraged.

"What do you mean, 'Dumb nigger'?" he roared.

In response the man hit Milt in the face. Two other guys jumped on Milt's back.

Like Bill Brown, Milt is a mild-mannered guy, but once this happened, he went into his Joe Palooka routine and methodically flattened all three of them. By this time the police had arrived, and all they could see was this huge man flattening all those people. One of the officers came up behind Milt and smacked him over the head with the largest flashlight I had ever seen. It didn't even phase Milt.

He just turned around and said, "Yes?"

The policeman stood there with his mouth hanging open, and then he began to laugh.

"I think I hit the wrong guy!"

Later, at the hospital, we presented a "game ball" to the nurse who assisted the doctor who sewed up Milt's skull.

The basketball team became a regular fixture throughout the Midwest during the off season. Sometimes we played as many as seventy-five games throughout Minnesota, North Dakota, South Dakota, Montana, Nebraska, Wisconsin, and Iowa. Week after week we travelled, meeting new people, spreading good will most of the time, and letting people see that we were really no different from the people with whom they worked and lived every day.

And, for the most part, we enjoyed ourselves.

It was January of 1972, and we were returning from our annual road trip to Montana. I was anxious to get home to Jan and the boys. I always thrived on the public life. But I also loved my family, and I could hardly wait to see them.

It was late the night when I arrived at our home in

Burnsville. I parked my car and headed for the door. Jan was
waiting for me.

"Hiya, babe!" I shouted. "It's been a long time!"

"Yes, it has, Karl."

"Jan, what's the matter?"

"Nothing now, Karl. I want you to take your things and
leave the house. I want a divorce."

"Aw, don't be ridiculous, Jan. Whatever it is, we can work it
out!"

"No, Karl. We can't. I don't love you anymore. I filed the
divorce papers while you were gone."

CHAPTER 26

Divorced

●

We were divorced in March, 1972. I was destroyed.

I had been so proud of Jan. We had our problems, though I had never thought they were serious enough to even consider a divorce. I always figured that they would work themselves out once Jan completed her education and was settled into a medical practice. I probably would be retiring from football before long, and life wouldn't have to continue at such a hectic pace. We'd become more of a "normal" family.

It's still painful to know I failed at something so important as marriage, though time has given me a much more healthy attitude toward Jan and made me see why our marriage failed.

The truth was that we were competing against each other, rather than working together. Our lives seldom overlapped. Looking back on it now, I can see that we were competing to see who was going to get "top billing." She had set her sights on becoming a respected, successful doctor. I had set mine on becoming the best strong safety in professional football, as well as on being a success in the dozen other ventures in which I was involved. Little time, or energy, was left for building a marriage.

Any marriage would be strained if even one of the partners was as dedicated to personal success as we both were. In our case, another complication was my over-involvement in everything I did and Jan's professional ambitions and growing disgust with my life as a Viking.

I handled everything, not just football, with reckless abandon and had way too many irons in the fire. In addition to playing for the Vikings and the community service and public appearances I enjoyed so thoroughly, there was my off-season job, the Vikings basketball team, and Sports Celebrities.

And the bars.

Denny Weber, a friend of mine who worked with a beer company in Mason City, Iowa, began talking one night about what a gold mine it would be for us to own a bar or two. "Kassulke, with your name and my experience, we could get rich."

We began our first bar in Mankato, for obvious reasons. With the Vikings' training camp there, it couldn't miss.

Before long we were doing well enough to invest in "Karl Kassulke's Bruiser's Bar" in Mason City, Iowa. Soon there followed a third one in Rochester, Minnesota.

Each had its successes, but they were plagued with fights and other problems I had to deal with personally. Also, I tried to make regular appearances in each bar. Business always picked up when the customers knew that I was going to be in town.

There just wasn't enough time left for the marriage.

Looking back today, I can see how mixed-up my priorities were. It wasn't that I didn't love my family. I really did. But the more Jan and I discussed our problems, the more obvious it was that what we both wanted in life was poles apart. She thought she shouldn't be married to a jock, and I thrived on my life in the public spotlight, both on and off the field; the conflict just never was resolved.

We were running to catch ourselves.

We found we were courting disaster.

I don't mean to sound smug, but there is a sense in which Jan did me a favor by divorcing me, though I certainly didn't see it at the time. I began to think more about who I was and what I really wanted out of life.

Because of that, I took time to find new ways of uplifting people. One of the most satisfying was to travel overseas to our servicemen in Korea and other places with Billy Kilmer of the Redskins and several other NFL players. I found great satisfaction and some fulfillment in helping my country in this way. And though my heart was broken and my two delightful sons were gone, I still clung to the thought: "At least I'm a *success*."

Only later would I think more deeply about what real success is.

Jan's decision to divorce me hadn't come out of the blue as much as it seemed that night. For some time we had been going to marriage counselors. She had never enjoyed the football life that much and had talked about its emptiness. She called it an "extended adolescence," and in a sense she was right. I knew it was much more though and tried to show her how I contributed to the welfare of people. There was more meaning to my life than just going around knocking people on the ground on a football field.

The previous summer, between her junior and senior years of medical school, she had asked me if she could study in Wales at the University of Cardiff. She felt that not only was the program important to her career, but she needed to get away for a while.

"Maybe it'll help our marriage, Karl. I'm just so confused and tired, and I need to get my head together."

"Fine. If you need some space, I'll give it to you."

So I took an advance in my salary from the Vikings, and we all headed for Wales, where I helped them get settled into a duplex in Cardiff. I headed back to Mankato and training camp where life became business as usual. Drills. Harrassing the rookies. Practices. Film sessions. The whole thing all over again.

When Jan and the boys returned, she seemed more relaxed, and I just assumed that the time away had helped to get her feelings under better control.

It didn't work out that way. Four months later she filed.

CHAPTER 27

Versailles

●

Going through that divorce was the most painful experience of my life—even including the accident. I've heard people say that a divorce is more traumatic than a spouse's death, an opinion that doesn't surprise me at all. I had never been known for my common sense and moderation, but after the divorce I really went off the deep end. My life ran to an even greater excess. At any time of the day or night I could be found drinking, smoking pot, picking up women, fighting. I was not a pretty sight to behold.

I was living my life for the Devil. I had been raised in a good home and knew better, but I just didn't care any more.

When I moved out of the house, a neighbor, Jim Mergens, introduced me to his brother, Paul. He and I moved into an apartment in the Versailles complex, just south of the football stadium. We lived there for about fifteen months, and our apartment became widely known as a place where there was usually a party in progress.

One night several of us guys had been playing cribbage and telling one story after another. About 3:00 A.M. we decided to take a swim. Down the hall we went and out to the pool in our birthday suits.

We were making an awful racket, and before long the manager came out to the pool to tell us to quiet down or get out of the pool. He nearly fainted when we all jumped out of the pool stark naked and took off for the apartment. He must have thought he'd be sued or something, because I could hear him moaning to himself, "What are they trying to do to me? Get me thrown in jail?"

We were in the kitchen making popcorn when there was a knock at the door. Without thinking, I opened it. It was a man from the gas company. He took one look at all of us standing around the apartment in the buff and gulped. "I've been called here to fix a gas leak. Where's it at?"

"I don't know. It sure isn't here. But come on in. We've got enough popcorn to feed a whole army." He accepted and nervously stepped in. It wasn't until later, after we'd all had a few beers and eaten most of the popcorn, that I began to realize what must have been going through the repairman's mind when he walked into an apartment full of nude men at three o'clock in the morning. I began to laugh.

"What's the matter with you, Kassulke?" he asked.

"Oh, I was just thinking about the look on your face when I opened the door."

"You know, I wasn't sure whether I should come in here or not," he chuckled. "Kassulke, you looked like a madman when you opened the door."

"That's why I only appear in public fully clothed," I informed him.

It was while I was living at the Versailles apartments that I met Monty Krizan. We soon became fast friends.

We both worked at the Left Guard, a restaurant in the Twin Cities area formed by Fuzzy Thurston and Max McGee of the Green Bay Packers and a local businessman named Bill Martini. It had been an old Piggly Wiggly supermarket, and they had redecorated it and covered the walls with blown-up photos of scenes from Vikings' games. It sat nearly seven hundred people and soon became the "in" place in the area.

I had been hired to be the celebrity host. My job was to mix with the patrons, slap a few backs, and make everyone feel welcome. It was a job for which I was perfectly qualified. I enjoyed meeting people, and the pleasure seemed to be mutual. The management even named a 22-ounce sirloin steak after me.

We hadn't been open that long when Larry, the manager, came in early one evening and told Monty he would have to quit. Monty had had some confrontations with an officer from one of the suburban police departments over a problem at his previous job, and the officer had used his friendship with another officer to get back at Monty.

I could overhear their argument, and I wouldn't keep out of it. "Wait a minute, Larry. You can't fire him like that. What you want him to quit for is nothing. The only difference is that this time you've got a cop on your case, and you're looking for a way out."

Larry glared at me. "Stay out of it, Karl."

"Stay out? Forget it! If Monty goes, I go. And then who is going to keep the people who come in here happy? Use your head, Larry. If there was anything wrong here, the police wouldn't be messing around with Monty. They'd come in and close down the place."

Monty and I won the argument, and before long it seemed as if we'd known each other all our lives. We were inseparable. After we closed down the Left Guard, some nights we would party until daybreak. Monty and I just hit it off, and we could have a better time with a bowl of popcorn and a six pack of Pepsi than most people could have blowing fifty dollars at a fancy restaurant. We were like little boys in a sandbox.

MONTY KRIZAN:

I can remember people walking up to Karl at the Left Guard and saying, "Say, Karl, I've got a son up at the Children's Hospital, and he's going to have a big operation in a couple of days. It'd sure be nice if you could drop by and see him. He'd really like that."

Karl would say, "Do you want to take your car or mine?"

"Oh? Uhh . . . I'll drive."

And he'd go. One minute the guy would ask him, and the next minute they would be going out the door. There wasn't anything Karl wouldn't do to help somebody.

When the divorce settlement came through in March of 1972, the judge had given Jan the right to use our house for fifteen months. He said that since I had paid for her entire medical education, I should get the house, but she would need it until she graduated from medical school and became established in her career. I agreed that it would be best for the boys to stay in their home.

Jan moved to her new residence in June of 1973, and I began my move back to the house in July. It took longer than expected.

We had decided to clean out the storage locker for the apartment first. Paul and I kept our motorcycles in the apartment so they wouldn't get stolen, and neither of us spent much time cleaning. So we both thought that it would be less depressing to begin with the locker.

We'd just gotten started when we found a box of old party decorations. This got Monty going, and while Paul and I loaded up Monty's van, he went back to the apartment and decorated the whole place.

Halloween witches and ghosts and skeletons. Valentine hearts. Thanksgiving turkeys. Christmas tinsel.

It took us three days just to get the first load out to the house!

By this time I was dating one of the young ladies who lived in our apartment building, and she had decided to move into a different apartment complex at the same time Paul and I were moving into my house. We agreed to help her. The trouble was that she lived on the third floor.

First, we brought some ropes and lowered a beautiful couch down the stairs. It must have taken us twenty minutes to get it out of there and into the van. As we walked back upstairs, an idea began to form in my mind.

"Monty, this is going to take us days if we have to keep going up and down all these stairs."

"I was thinking the same thing, Karl."

"I tell you what. We'll take turns throwing her stuff off the balcony and catching it. How about it?"

Monty was as crazy as I was, so he agreed.

"But who's going to do the throwing first?" We decided to flip a coin. I won.

When I walked into her apartment, the first thing I spotted were her mattresses leaning against the wall. I picked up one of the mattresses and carried it out to the balcony. Monty had run into my apartment to get my motorcycle helmet and some leather gloves, and he was waiting for me.

"Geronimo!"

Poor guy. That mattress nearly killed him.

After that, we carried the heavy items down the stairs and threw the light ones off the balcony.

In the meantime, the party was still going on downstairs. I had never seen half those people before in my life, but anybody was welcome at my place. Whenever we decided to load up the van, we would give everyone at the party an armload of junk from the apartment. Before long, the van would be filled. Then we'd spend the rest of the evening playing cribbage, eating popcorn, and drinking.

Finally, there was only one more large item to move. My waterbed. We didn't know how to drain it. We looked all around it for a way to get all that water out, but to no avail. Finally, we decided that since my apartment was on the ground floor, we'd just roll it out the bedroom door, push it down the hall to the patio, and cut it open.

The fact that we had been partying for several days didn't help matters any. We couldn't get that mattress out of its frame. Part of it would roll toward the edge, but never quite enough. Monty finally climbed into the box, put his feet against the frame, and started pushing. I was on the other side of the bed, pulling with all my strength.

Every time we'd just about get it out of the bed one of us would start laughing, and I'd lose my grip.

Take my word for it. You haven't seen anything until you've seen a waterbed throw a 180-pound man clear across a room and against the wall. We'd both lie there and laugh ourselves silly. Then we'd get up enough strength to try it again. Finally, the mattress ruptured and began to spurt water all over the room.

"Cripes, Karl. The whole bedroom's going to be drowned!"

"Quick! Run into the bathroom and get some towels."

We barricaded the door with towels, the throw rug from the kitchen, and everything else we could find.

"At least it'll only be this room that gets drenched."

In the meantime, Monty had torn off the window screen and was bailing out the water with a dish pan. Finally we were convinced that we had gotten rid of enough water that we could drag it outside. But by the time we actually got it out of the apartment there was water everywhere.

But we did get moved. Finally.

CHAPTER 28

Grand View Lodge

●

As long as I can remember, I have loved to fish. I've made it a rule never to miss an opportunity.

I was working at the Left Guard one noon when one of the waitresses talked to me about attending a parade in her home town. "All you have to do, Karl, is go up there and ride in the Fourth of July parade, and you get the whole weekend for free."

It sounded great.

Later, I walked over to the bar where Monty was mixing drinks. "You want to go fishing this weekend?"

"You bet! But where?"

"Well, I've got this deal all worked out. Everything is free. All we have to do is go up there and ride in the parade on the Fourth. You know, be a part of the celebration. And we get to stay there for nothing."

"Great! Where is it?"

"Grand View Lodge."

"Where's that?"

"Brainerd. On Gull Lake."

On Friday afternoon we got our clothes packed up in rolls. Monty borrowed Paul Mergen's motorcycle, and we were off.

We went up through Buffalo on Highway 25, stopping to have a beer or two in several of the small towns along the way. We drove rather foolishly, running up and down road ditches and country dirt roads. By the time we got to Brainerd we were covered with dirt from head to toe.

Once there we stopped at a bar near Paul Bunyan Land. We hadn't even finished our first beer when somebody recognized my laugh and came over to the table.

"You're Karl Kassulke, aren't you?"

"Guilty as charged!"

Before long there were twenty or thirty people over in the corner with us. We were all having a good time when someone asked, "Hey, what're you guys doing up here, anyway?"

"Don't you know? We're riding in the parade on the Fourth."

"Well, I'll be!" He looked puzzled.

Monty leaned over to me and said, "Karl, I think maybe you should call the resort and see if everything's OK. Everybody seems a little surprised to see us."

Given my poor memory, he wanted to be sure that I had remembered things right. So I went out to the phone booth and called the lodge. They told me that everything was great, and there was a cabin we could have.

By the time we found the Grand View Lodge and checked in, it was late. Several people were waiting for us, and we all went into the bar and sat talking late into the night.

What a weekend!

We swam. Fished. Slept late. Took part in a water carnival. Rode in the parade. Showed Vikings' highlight films. Signed autographs. Laughed. Told stories.

Monty kept after me to work out. It would be only a few weeks until the Vikings' training camp, and he felt like he owed it to me to help me get in shape. We had brought our running shoes along, and every morning he'd get me out and make me run. Monty was a faster sprinter than I was, but I could whip him on endurance every time. We'd run till we got sick from all the drinking the night before, or until we had sweated most of it out of our system.

One morning we were coming by the lodge when Monty said, "Hey, they're going to serve lunch in ten minutes. We better get showered and up there fast, or we'll miss out."

I issued the challenge.

"Monty, I'll bet you a bottle of J & B that I can shower and get dressed and over to lunch before you can."

"You're on!"

We took off through the trees and cabins at full gallop,

pulling off our shirts and nearly tearing the screen door off its hinges when we got to the cabin. Clothes went flying in every direction, and we went running down the hallway with nothing on but our socks. We both hit the doorway at the same time and knocked it clean off its hinges.

The shower was one of those metal ones, about two feet square. We both wedged in there and were trying to shampoo our hair and lather the sweat off our bodies when I began to laugh.

"Knock it off, Karl!"

I couldn't help it. It was one of those crazy situations that I always seemed to find, and before I realized what was happening, my foot slipped and we both fell down. The whole shower buckled under, over, and around us.

Now the shower stood four rather than seven feet high. We couldn't get out. Monty tried to turn the water off, and it wouldn't turn off completely. So we also got scalded.

The racket must have been something else, because soon we heard the outside door opening and voices. One of the maids, probably still in high school, poked her head around the doorway. Her face turned ghostly white.

Poor kid. It must have been a sight. Two grown men, with nothing on but their socks, pinned inside a busted shower and laughing so hard they couldn't get out.

On our last morning in Brainerd, we ran our bikes through the back roads, something I always enjoyed doing. The quick corners and turns made the ride exciting.

As we came around one curve, we saw a boat being backed across the road. There was no time to stop, so Monty went to the left ditch and I went to the right. Unfortunately, there was a log lying in the right ditch, and my bike flipped me up into the air and out into the swamp by the side of the road.

Money. Credit cards. Receipts. All of them flew everywhere. So did a large flock of ducks.

I was lying in mud, my clothes were torn, and I had a few scratches. Monty must have thought I had been killed.

"Karl! Karl! Are you all right?"

He was running through the mud looking for me. I pretended to be unconscious.

When he saw me he groaned, "Oh, no!"

I couldn't take it any longer and began to laugh. Before long we were in the middle of a furious mud fight. We were laughing and throwing mud at one another as fast as we could grab it, and the people who were watching us from the road must have thought we were nuts.

Once we picked up what we could find of my things, we rode into town on Monty's bike and rented a truck to take mine back to Minneapolis. Monty rode alongside the truck. It was a warm day, and as we headed south from St. Cloud, I pulled over to pick up a boy standing by the road. I figured that he wasn't big enough to give me too much trouble.

We had a great time, laughing and telling stories most of the way. He told me he was going to a party in Coon Rapids, which was right on our way. Just before we got there I asked him what he'd been doing up north.

"Oh, nothing much."

"What do you mean by that?"

"Well, I just took off from the reformatory."

I didn't want to know any more. I told him I'd drop him off at his party if he didn't tell anyone how he'd gotten there.

Once we got the truck back to U-Haul and took our showers, we headed to the Left Guard to eat. The waitress who had arranged for our weekend was on duty and just glared at me.

"Monty, do you suppose we did something wrong while we were in Brainerd?"

"I don't know. Maybe her dad had to pay for that shower we wrecked."

I walked over to talk with her.

"Kathy, what's the matter with you? What did we do wrong?"

"Kassulke, do you know that my father held up the Fourth of July parade for two hours waiting for you? And you never even showed up."

"What are you talking about? We were there!"

"What do you mean, you were there? Where were you?"

"Just where you told us. The Grand View Lodge in Brainerd."

She began to laugh.

"Can't you get anything right, Karl? You were supposed to be at the Grand View Lodge in Alexandria!"

I never said I was perfect.

CHAPTER 29

Denial

●

"I don't want any more motorcycles in training camp. I mean it. One of you guys could get hurt on those doggone things."

I had laughed when Bud said that.

Paul Mergens and I had just gotten settled into my Burnsville home, and with Monty taking over my Mankato bar, the future looked great. I was on top of the world.

I never expected anything to stop me. Least of all, a motorcycle. But once it happened, it became a matter of getting my life going again.

When I was brought battered and bleeding into Methodist Hospital, I was unconscious. The doctors doubted that I'd make it through the first night. It was several days before they were sure I'd live.

Dr. Dick Siebert, Jr., son of the University of Minnesota baseball coach, was on duty at the time, along with Dr. Paul Blake. The papers quoted Dr. Siebert as saying that anyone who had not been in the physical condition I was in probably couldn't have survived the injury.

All I know is that I suffered several broken bones and a severe head injury. My spine was fractured at the seventh thoracic vertebra, and my sixth and seventh vertebrae were crushed. Later a decompression laminectomy was performed to remove the bone chips and fuse the two vertebrae together.

The accident happened on Tuesday, and by Thursday my condition had improved so much that I was placed on the critical list. I stayed in critical condition for another twelve days and made it to serious by August 7.

My condition didn't help the spirit of the Vikings' training camp. Bud Grant said that it was the worst training camp he ever experienced. The rumors about my condition were flying everywhere. "He's better." "He's worse." "He's dying."

My friends were all very upset, of course, and it was difficult for the coaches to get the veterans to concentrate on their training. Finally, Bud told the team to ignore all the rumors. He would talk personally with the doctors every day and announce my condition at the evening meal.

Bud had heard that I'd been hurt before he left for camp in Mankato, but he hadn't realized how serious it was until Jim Finks called him. That night he had the team assemble and informed them that I wasn't expected to live through the night.

When Bud asked the men to spend some time together in prayer for me, I am told that there were few men in the room who weren't weeping.

It's hard for me to write about this particular period of my life, because most of what I know is what other people tell me. But I do want to thank everyone who was praying for me in those days. At the time, I certainly wasn't living in a relationship with God that would have caused me to pray, but I really do believe that God answered the prayers that so many people sent.

For a long time the doctors were concerned about my head injury more than they were about my spine. It was of such severity that the doctors couldn't believe I had been wearing a helmet. For weeks my attention span was fifteen to twenty seconds at most. And then it was back to dreamland.

I had a terrible time accepting that I would never walk again. Surely with all the wonders of modern science, the doctors would be able to get me well. If they would just hurry it up a bit, I might be able to catch the end of training camp.

I refused to believe that I'd have to spend the rest of my life in a wheelchair. I absolutely refused to believe it. I thought that I could just make up my mind to walk again, and some day I'd be able to get up out of that bed and do it.

I now understand that my frustration was a combination of my denial of the situation and what the doctors call "organic brain syndrome." Every day they had to tell me the same thing, and every day I would argue with them.

"I'm gonna walk, I tell you. I will!"

Then I'd drift into semi-consciousness.

And two hours later it would start all over again.

MONTY KRIZAN:

It was painful to watch Karl and realize that someone's foolish mistake could take a man's legs away from him and cause him all that suffering. We were both very lucky to be alive, but it was tough to forget the loss.

After Karl began to get better, he was preoccupied with getting to training camp. I'd wheel my chair into his room, and he'd say, "Monty, look in my locker and see if my pants are in there."

I'd look. "Yeah, Karl. They're here."

"Get 'em out for me, and let's get out of here."

"Come on, Karl. We can't do that."

"Sure we can. Look! This bed will stand up. You can make it do that. C'mon, help me!"

I was in a wheelchair with broken arms and legs and could hardly get around myself. And Karl wanted me to get him out of bed and escape the place! I can't imagine anyone ever having more courage and determination to live than he had.

He was so messed up. So hurt. But to himself he wasn't hurt at all. He was just impaired for the moment and needed fixing here and there. He really thought he'd do a lot better if they'd just let him out of the hospital.

I sure wish he had his legs. But I'll take him just the way he is. The world would be a lot less joyful if he weren't around to keep us all smiling.

Those early weeks in Methodist Hospital were filled with pain and frustration. I had such difficulty remembering what had happened a few minutes earlier, to say nothing of what had happened one or two days before. It seemed as if I spent the whole time in utter confusion. My mind is still very vague about those weeks, except for that feeling of confusion. After listening to my friends' descriptions of my suffering and mental anguish, I feel very fortunate not to be able to chart my progress for myself.

My friend, Jim Klobuchar of *The Minneapolis Star,* wrote several columns describing my condition. His column in mid-August of 1973 describes my condition quite well, much better than I could do. I share it with you, with thanks both to *The Star* and Jim.

HE'S TOUCHED DOWN . . . CAN HE REACH UP?

Once in a while Karl Kassulke will reach into a vase of flowers, laboriously remove one of the blossoms with his splinted hand and give it to the nurse.

His lips will form a smile and he may say something like "I'm measuring you for a bouquet."

It is a thin, toneless remnant of the convulsive Karl Kassulke giggles that would announce one of his clubhouse putdowns.

No matter how faint or tentative, however, it is a flicker of his old personality.

And his attendants and closest friends who witness it want to cheer the discovery.

There is no place for story book illusions in the Methodist Hospital room where the 32-year-old football player lies with his legs in paralysis and his mind drifting between worlds—the one of the Huckleberry Finn athlete that is lost to him forever and the other inert and alien, a hospital bed from which he raises and lowers his encased arms as though grappling with reality.

His recognitions are growing. But there are still voids in his memory that doctors themselves can only guess at.

He has been told he probably will not walk again, so that he might understand the enormity of the battle he faces and so there will be no new emotional shock.

It is not clear that he fully comprehends this as one of the realities, or that he has yet accepted. His athlete's instincts may be resisting it.

They have said these things before, to Ben Hogan and others.

But he speaks no heroic defiance. His struggle is in his eyes. He will focus on his visitor for interludes and respond by speaking if it is one of those hours when he is alert and communicative. And then he will turn his head, as though trying to shut off what he is beginning to understand, and let silence restore the old world.

The nurse leaned down to him to announce a visitor. "An old friend," she said, "who would like to say hello." He recognized the name and made an effort at jocularity. "Tell him I think it would be acceptable," he said to the nurse.

His voice was low and formless, but he seemed composed and courteous and the visitor had to resist the impulse to cuff him on the chin and to give him one of those shaggy clubhouse salutations not normally registered with the nurses' office.

Karl would almost demand it in the other days. He was boisterous and guffawing—a rampaging, big-hearted locker room clown. Yes, he was a competent and totally fearless football player. But it was Karl the human being that attracted people to him in swarms, the kids on the playground where he would come to teach football, the swells at the supper club bar.

In many ways he was an athletic roustabout, a child of nature so supremely exuberant in the life of a successful football player and gypsy musketeer he could not see it would mean the destruction of his marriage.

He had brooded about that, but he still loved his two children and he never tried to alibi his own responsibility for what happened. For all of his horse-play he was the essence of the man's man, and as an athlete it was never more evident than in his willingness to absorb injury and to play with it. Like most tough guys in the NFL, he developed a casual familiarity with pain. Kassulke's pain threshold went a step beyond. He was almost congenial with pain.

But when you went on the injured waiver lists in pro football, there was always next month.

He lay on his hospital bed last night with no feeling in his legs and only distant, sometimes unconnected recollections. He was uncovered from the waist up. His upper body looked strong and his face was unmarked.

"A lot of the people you played against have asked about you," the visitor said. He named some of the pro football stars Kassulke had competed with. Karl nodded and began to turn away. His visitor touched his arm and Karl's eyes came back.

"I feel alright," he said. "Better. I feel better. Maybe you want to finish my supper, though."

His plate of chicken and potatoes and peas was barely tasted. Beside his bed was a picture of his two young sons wrestling with a football. A half dozen vases and baskets of flowers touched up the room. There were cards, but no suggestions of the 400 to 500 messages a day the hospital has been receiving from people inquiring about him or wanting to see him.

It may be weeks or months before his view of his condition is clear enough to allow him normal visiting periods. The doctors have removed him from the critical list, but it is plain that his real struggle for rehabilitation from his motorcycle injury of July 24 is yet to begin.

There is some small indication that the spinal damage he received may not be as severe as first believed, but this is speculative and the present medical concensus is that Karl has lost the use of his legs permanently.

"Yet there is still the human equation," said Dr. John Baumgartner, one of his attending doctors, himself a former University of Minnesota football player. "Other people have come back when it was said they would never walk again. It may be too early to ascertain if he has any real chance for that from a strictly medical reading.

"It is also too early to say whether any of Karl's retentive powers will be permanently affected. But there has been a strong improvement this week from where he was last week."

Daily he receives visits from his roommate, Paul Mergens, to whom he responds with his greatest warmth and animation. Occasionally Mergens tries to coax him into a mock contest of arm-wrestling.

He speaks little of football.

Perhaps it is the subject he is resisting. He drifted momentarily last night and said in a kind of aside, "Just not young enough to play football anymore."

And then he turned once more to his visitor, and he suddenly seemed very intense. "I've got to get the program together," he said. "It's coming."

He had the sound of an athlete getting ready.*

*Jim Klobuchar, "He's Touched Down . . . Can He Reach Up?" *The Minneapolis Star,* August 16, 1973. Copyright © 1973 by *The Minneapolis Star.* Reprinted with permission.

CHAPTER 30

Rehab Four

●

On September 5, I was moved to the University of Minnesota Rehabilitation Hospital. I could never have anticipated the ways in which that hospital would change my life.

When the ambulance carrying me arrived at the fourth-floor entrance on Church Street, the place was filled with people. Television reporters. Newspaper people. Photographers. Doctors. Nurses. The just curious. Even a couple of Vikings.

I waved to them all as the attendants rushed me inside.

I was exhausted by the pandemonium. I was weak from having had no physical activity for weeks, and with all the excitement I had not slept well the night before.

Before long a pretty, long-haired young nurse came bustling through the door and began to chase the reporters and cameramen out into the hall. When she finished, she came back into the room. My parents were still talking to me, and she obviously didn't know who they were.

"I'm sorry, folks. But you're really going to have to leave. It's getting late, and I have a lot of work to do with Karl yet tonight."

Dad shrugged his shoulders and said, "C'mon, Leona. It's getting late, and we need to get something to eat."

I tried to focus my mind on this lovely creature who was checking my pulse and temperature, but my eyes kept blurring and I felt more than a little disoriented.

"Hi, Karl. My name is Sue. I will be your primary care nurse and will be overseeing your care and rehabilitation here. This will include physical therapy to help you regain your strength. You will also be seen by orthopedic doctors for your leg injury.

And later on you'll have occupational therapy. You will probably be here for a couple of months."

"Then will I be able to play for the Vikings again?"

"I don't think so, Karl, but we will help you make new plans based on your interests and abilities. Do you have any other questions?"

"Sure."

"What?"

"You want to mess around?"

She blushed like a schoolgirl and gave me the best brush-off I've ever received.

"Why, Karl, I'd love to! But no, not on company time!"

We both began to laugh like little kids. I knew I'd found another friend. She would be no pushover.

My routine was rather involved.

I'd be awakened between 6:30 and 7:00 in the morning by the night nurse and dressed in street clothes. Nobody wore hospital gowns or whites on the rehabilitation floor. The idea was that they weren't treating sick people. Rather, they were treating well people who were disabled. That philosophy helped us all and was reflected in everything that happened. With none of the staff walking around with long faces, their positive attitude rubbed off on the patients.

We all ate breakfast together in the dining room, family style, with four to eight people at each table.

After breakfast we were sent over to the physical therapy wing, then to the occupational therapy area. If a person felt particularly low, a counselor was always available. In fact, when I was first admitted, I had to visit one every day. Later, all I had to do was ask to see a counselor, and one would be available later in the day.

We put in full days but in the evenings had free time for pool, ping pong, cribbage, and singing in the lounge. There was a television there, too. We weren't allowed to stay in our rooms in the evening but were required to mix with one another and get better acquainted. Thus, some of the more depressed individuals came into contact with the more exuberant people like myself, and sooner or later everyone would manage to break through their private pains.

As I said, our schedules were full. Our days gave us no chance to succumb to one of the real dangers a paraplegic faces—inactivity. It leads so quickly to depression.

Some people think that occupational therapy involves activities like basket weaving and needlepoint. Maybe it's that way at some places, but it wasn't for us. The therapists helped us work through our anxieties about what we might be able to do once we were out of the hospital and also taught us how to recover dexterity in the use of our hands.

One helpful device developed there was a hydraulic lift that fit under our buttocks and lifted us to a standing position while we did our work. Our leg bones were forced to bear our weight and thus any bone deterioration that might normally happen was dramatically slowed.

I still believed I'd be able to walk again.

That was all the motivation I needed to work vigorously at the physical therapy program. I couldn't say that I was excited by the exercises, but they did keep me busy and kept my mind off my problems. By September 20 I was able to lift twenty-pound weights with each arm!

The doctors also wanted me to rebuild my upper torso strength. Eventually when I became more mobile, this part of my body would have to move me from place to place. These goals made me work on my physical therapy with enthusiasm.

Almost any movement caused me to perspire. For some reason, the injury interfered with my normal temperature regulating mechanism; and from the point of my injury down, I was unable to perspire. All such release came through my chest and head. Jeanne Kogl, my physical therapist, teased me that I could sweat while reading a book. It was almost that bad.

My progress was slow at first. I had several broken bones, and for some time my right calf had styman pins sticking through it to hold the bones in place. Those pins extended about eight inches beyond each side of the leg, and they made my transfers from bed to wheelchair and chair to bed very awkward. As a result, much of my physical therapy had to be delayed until the bones in my right leg healed.

Every day they put me through "range of motion" exercises. Range of motion is simply the putting of one's extremities through their normal movements. People whose muscles function properly are able to do this themselves. Those of us who are paralyzed do it passively. That is, someone helps us until we learn to do it for ourselves. This keeps our joints flexible and prevents the contractions of our muscles that would eventually make us deformed.

Just as important were the transfers I had to learn to make. Basically, they included wheelchair to floor and back. Wheelchair to car, and car to wheelchair. Wheelchair to bed and back. And wheelchair to bath. Eventually, all of these had to be completed with no assistance.

Floor transfers were the most difficult to learn. I would have thought that the tub transfer would be the worst because of the slipperiness, but the buoyancy of the water and the handles around tubs (like soap dishes) make it quite easy. In fact, I can probably scamper out of a tub as fast as most people!

The floor was something else. I had to learn how to hold the chair in a way that it wouldn't come toppling over on my head while I was pulling myself up and turning around to sit down. While I was practicing, the chair did get me more than once. The first time it happened I was really scared, but as my upper body strength improved I felt better about my ability to cope with my problems. Soon I learned how to fall without getting hurt. The therapist, Jeanne Kogl, and I would just laugh, and I would try again.

Once I learned to master that transfer, I was ready for anything.

That skill has come in handy on more than one occasion since leaving the hospital. Now that I live at home, I usually use the couch as an intermediate step to the chair, but occasionally I have been caught in situations where I had to transfer from the ground to the chair.

The most notable was the day I slipped off the seat while reaching for the mail. Not only was it embarrassing to fall, but the chair rolled about thirty feet. I had to crawl the whole distance on my elbows, and I was very grateful that I had learned my lesson well!

I hadn't been there long before I realized that Sue Scipioni was a special kind of person. I just felt good whenever she was around. Before long, she and I were having as much fun as Hack and I had had at training camp.

She usually requested the 3 to 11 shift in order to be with the patients more. That was fine with me. She would do the extra things most people wouldn't even think of doing for their patients.

Like cooking spaghetti and rigatoni for the whole floor. Sue would come in early before her shift started, and my resident doctor, Tom Szymke, would help her. We'd all eat until we were stuffed, and I could feel the change in attitude on the floor every time she did it. We were all encouraged.

Because we were basically well people with disabilities, the atmosphere on the floor really depended on the patients. I did my best to keep things moving.

First were the drag races down the halls. Two young men, Roger Christiansen from Prescott, Wisconsin, and Scott Johnson from Hutchinson, Minnesota, especially enjoyed this form of entertainment. Everyone would get out into the hall, and we'd take turns challenging one another. This went on for several weeks until an administrator heard about it and made us stop.

"Karl, if one of you guys couldn't stop and went flying down the stairs, we could have a terrible lawsuit on our hands."

He was right, of course. But every once in a while we would sneak a race or two in anyway.

One night Bob Niemi, a senior nursing assistant who became a good friend, was standing by my bed talking with me when I had another idea. "Bob, do the doctors keep those exam gloves in the main supply room?"

After he affirmed my suspicion and left the room, I transferred to my wheelchair and was off on my way to the supply room. I must have "borrowed" fifty of them.

We used them in every conceivable manner. Most often we would fill them with water, tie them like balloons, and paint fingernails and hair on them. I carried one with me wherever I went; and nearly every night I'd take the elevator upstairs to Rehab Five, the children's floor, and entertain a room of kids with my balloon people.

It was tough to watch those kids. Some of them had been deformed at birth, and others had been injured. I tried to at least help lift their spirits, and soon came to love them. They had so much courage, and the truth is, they cheered me at least as much as I cheered them.

But the gloves weren't always used for such constructive purposes. Occasionally we would start water balloon fights with them or wheel around the floor holding down every finger but the middle one and giving everyone the bird. All sorts of nonsense.

One night Sue was reading to me. I was having trouble sleeping, which happened frequently, and she was staying late with me. About one o'clock, Roger, one of my roommates, got tied up in his sheets and was falling out of bed.

"Hey," I asked. "Do you need a hand?"

"Yeah." He was caught halfway between the floor and his bed.

So I threw one of my hand people at him. His whole bed was drenched. We were all laughing so hard, we woke up half the floor! And before long we had one of the best water fights we had the whole time I was there.

I felt that since we were all in the same boat and probably none of us would ever walk again, we should try to learn to make the best of it. In view of how easy it was to become depressed about our future—and there were moments of awful despair—we really needed some silliness in our lives. So many of the guys couldn't get over their grief for their lost mobility, and our sessions with the therapists weren't enough in themselves to give us the positive attitudes we needed about ourselves. What better way to learn a positive attitude than by being together?

And our silliness was part of it.

We all had our problems. But we could make a go of it.

CHAPTER 31

My Day

●

They called it Karl Kassulke Day. I'll never be able to say "thank you" enough.

Paul Flatley and Joe Duffy started it.

As I lay in the hospital, the bills kept mounting, and before long all my personal and NFL insurance coverage was gone. In my state of mind I had been blissfully unaware of the problem, but my friends knew what was happening.

Many of the Vikings and other friends had kept in contact with me at the hospital. I wouldn't dare mention names, because I know I'd forget some of them. But the guys were wonderful to me. They'd come over after practice and play cribbage some nights, and other nights they'd just stop by to see how I was doing. I was so fortunate to have such loyal friends.

On October 30, the medical staff at the hospital let me take my first trip to the stadium. It was my first opportunity to be with the team at practice since the accident, and I was like a kid waiting for Santa Claus. When the day finally arrived, Bobby Bryant and Bob Lurtsema picked me up at the Church Street entrance of the hospital.

It was a taste of heaven on earth. I had seen the game on TV that Sunday, but what a thrill it was to be able to watch the films with the guys and offer my words of wisdom and encouragement.

"You sure blew it that time, Eller!"

"Haw, Bobby. You've got to learn how to cover those wide receivers on the sideline!"

We traded our insults back and forth. It was like old times all over again. I'd enjoyed the game on TV, but this was like coming back to life!

184

When I got back to the hospital, I told Sue all about it. Sue was a perky, no-nonsense gal from Bovey, Minnesota, and was fresh out of college. I tried to shock her with my ribald tales of what had happened at the stadium. She was embarrassed, as usual, but she refused to let me get the best of her.

"Karl, you're not that funny. And if you don't knock it off, I'm not going to give you your shower tonight!"

Now that was a punishment more than I could bear.

"I'll be good. I promise."

I don't quite know how to say this, but by this time there was more to our relationship than simply nurse and patient. It had been very embarrassing to both of us when she first had been assigned to give me my shower. For the first few weeks, Bob Niemi usually assisted me with this because of my awkward transfers. But it was actually the primary nurse's responsibility to help each of her patients.

Because of our growing friendship, my shower had become the source of a great deal of interest among both patients and staff. It was like the Rookie Show all over again, only this time I was the victim.

As we headed for the shower someone would begin to sing "Behind Closed Doors."

But we always kept it very correct and proper. Well, almost. I kept after Sue to give me a smooch. She'd say, "Not on company time, Karl!"

It was maddening.

"Company time, nuts! I wanna smooch!"

Before long we would be laughing and singing and carrying on so loud that some of the other guys would come into the shower room and join us.

With all modesty, then, I must say that my shower was frequently the social event of the evening on our floor! And of course we teased Susan unmercifully.

The shower stalls were quite small, and by getting in there with me (and yes, I did cover myself to the point of decency) to help me wash my back and feet, she ended up soaked by the time we finished.

She concocted an unusual uniform to protect herself. First she would take two small plastic bags and put them over her shoes, securing them with rubber bands. Then she would take a huge plastic garbage bag, cut holes for her head and arms, and pull it over her clothes. To make her uniform complete, she would use one of my t-shirts to hold the bag in place.

Ravishing!

Somehow I feel she never believed me when I told her how beautiful she looked. I had a special t-shirt with the word "Puma" written across the front. It soon became Susan's. We labeled her "The Grand Puma."

"Watch out, you guys, The Grand Puma is in a bad mood tonight."

It took time, but she learned to appreciate our crude attempts at humor.

I first learned of what Joe Duffy was doing when he came in to visit me one day. "Karl, I want you to shut your mouth and listen for once. No arguments, alright?"

"If you say so."

"Karl, there are a number of us who are concerned about the way your medical bills are piling up, and we'd like to do something about it."

"But Joe, I couldn't expect you to pay any of my bills."

"Karl, I said 'No arguments.' Paul Flatley and I have decided to put something together, and all we want from you is your okay. We think the people of Minnesota would welcome the opportunity to contribute to your expenses, and we'd like to do a benefit for you this fall. There won't be any manipulation or begging. We'll just announce that because your bills have mounted so fast, we're going to ask people to contribute what they'd like. Something for the Hunkie!"

I agreed to his idea. In fact, I thanked him. I could see that I would need help with the bills.

They set it up for November 25. The Chicago Bears would

be in town. That was fine with me. I always loved kicking the Bears' tails.

Later, I asked Sue if she'd like to come to the game with me. She blushed like a teen-ager asked out for her first date. It was high school all over again.

November 25th was a great day for a ball game. The best part was that we whipped the Bears 31–13. My whole family was given a private box on the west side of the stadium. Just before halftime, Mom, Dad, and my sisters, Carmen, Chris, and Kathy, accompanied me down the elevator to the stadium basement. Joe ushered us through the locker room tunnel.

As the guys came off the field at halftime, they all kept shaking my hand and telling me how good it was to see me. It felt great to be back there.

I wasn't prepared for what happened next. The Vikings band was playing the song "Ramblin' Man" as Jim Marshall, Bill Brown, and Grady Alderman wheeled me out onto the field.

All those people!

I'd forgotten what it was like in that place when it was full. Because it was my first public appearance in a wheelchair, I also felt more than a little self-conscious. I was expectant, and terrified.

The crowd began to cheer. Then they stood. I could feel the tears beginning to roll down my cheeks. They were cheering for me. For Hunkie!

I could hear people yelling out words of encouragement.

"Hang in there, Karl."

"We love you."

It was amazing. They just kept standing and cheering, and I didn't know what to do. I turned to look at my teammates. They had tears in their eyes, too.

I motioned to Jim, and he bent over to where I sat. "Are they going to do this much longer?"

"I hope so, Hunkie," he said. "I hope so."

And they did.

Governor Wendell Anderson was there and proclaimed it Karl Kassulke Day. Hubert Humphrey spoke, as did Grady, Bill, and Jim. And Bud. And Max Winter, the owner of the Vikings.

When Joe announced the amount of money that had been collected, I couldn't believe my ears. Over $175,000! As it turned out, the total would eventually approach a quarter million. The money was put into a trust fund to be used for rehabilitation and medical costs.

"Joe, please let me tell them thanks."

He wouldn't hand the mike to me. "Karl, I think you've had enough for one day."

He was right. I was exhausted and could barely keep my composure. And I was feeling more than overwhelmed.

As the players came back out on the field, my old buddies came over to talk to me before the second half started. I told them how much I would appreciate their beating the Bears.

I simply cannot express my gratitude deeply enough. It was a wonderful day, and I wish that I could personally thank everyone who reached out to help me at that time.

I want everyone to know how much I love them for remembering ol' Kassulke.

CHAPTER 32

Home at Last

●

I was released from the University of Minnesota Rehabilitation Hospital on January 18. The thought of being home had been on my mind for so long, and now the time had finally come.

Actually, I had been going out of the hospital on a doctor's pass for some time. Usually, it was for an evening on the town with Monty or Paul. Monty and I would go to Momma D's. After eating in a hospital for months, it was a special treat. Monty and I would eat until we were convinced that we couldn't get another bite in our mouths. And then Momma D would bring out some more.

At the time, I was wearing a special brace that was designed to protect my spine where it had been shattered. It laced up the front like an old-fashioned corset. No way was I going to Momma D's with that brace tied like the doctors wanted. By the time our meal was half finished I would have it untied.

They gave me a weekend pass at Christmas, too. Paul Mergens came to get me. Sue had made a list of instructions that looked like a grocery list, telling him what he should and should not do. He followed them to the letter. I couldn't talk him out of any of them.

Sue even borrowed her brother's car and came out to see me one afternoon. When she came in the door, I realized how much her coming meant to me, but I still wasn't able to talk with her about it. I felt that I had nothing to offer her. She was a healthy, energetic beautiful woman, and I was a broken down, crippled ex-jock.

It was also Paul who brought me home when I went there for good. Paul is one of those special people in my life. We lived together before the accident, and he stayed with me for over a year after I came home—at a great personal financial loss—and took excellent care of me. Several times every night he had to get up to turn me over so I wouldn't get pressure sores. Never a complaint or even a hint did I ever hear to suggest that he was less than happy in helping me.

And he wouldn't take anything for his help.

Paul also tried to help manage the bar in Rochester. By this time all my bars were in deep financial trouble, and he quit his job to do what he could to help get matters corrected. We never did, and eventually I had to sell them all at a loss. I came out on the wrong end of the stick to the tune of about $100,000.

Living at my home was another problem. Not only did I have all those negative memories from my marriage to deal with, but the house was a split-level one that required my moving up and down stairs nearly every time I did anything. I needed help getting to the family room. Then to the kitchen. Then to the bathroom. Upstairs. Downstairs. It was the pits.

Paul couldn't be there all the time, and my sister, Carmen, who had come to stay and help me, had errands of her own. The days became very frustrating and quite lonely. I had always been so active, and now I was almost completely dependent on others. It was also terribly humiliating at first, and it goes without saying that I was always a proud person.

Those months I spent in the Burnsville house were the lowest point of my life. In some ways living there was even worse than being in the hospital. At least there I had kept busy and had spent time with other people like myself. When I was low, there had been someone to talk with there; and I could take my mind off myself by helping others.

At home I just felt lost. It was like there was no purpose in living any longer. Not that I wanted to die. But there was nothing really important for me to *do*. I had enough income coming in from my NFL pension so that my basic needs were met. My frustration came from much deeper personal concerns than merely money. I just couldn't feel like I was making an important contribution anymore.

I responded by getting back in the fast track again, trying to drown my problems in drinking and partying—smiling and laughing on the outside, but dying on the inside. Without a point in living, my self-esteem was at an all-time low. I felt useless and unwanted, even though I continued to put on a good front. Whatever the pain, I just couldn't bring myself to talk about it with anyone.

I would not have become the complete person I am today if it hadn't been for Susan. I could level with her. She came out to the house to see me nearly every day. By then she had bought a new car for the twenty-mile trip and was driving me to many fun places.

She would come to the door, and I'd say, "Let's get out of here. I don't like this place." And off we would go. Sometimes we'd go to a park. Sometimes we'd just drive around town. Sometimes we'd go to a drive-in movie. And we would talk and talk and talk.

And eat popcorn!

I still hadn't learned, though, to deal with people's kind intentions. I was grateful for the help people gave me, but the feeling of degradation was still there. I had been so independent, and now people had to carry me up and down the stairs wherever I went. I had lost my independence. Also, my memory was still weak, and I became easily confused about where I was or what had happened just moments earlier—or the day before.

About all I was living for was a good time. But even the partying and drinking were beginning to wear thin. I went back to my old job at the Left Guard, and everyone I met seemed to want to talk about how great it had been in the good old days. It was as if the only way people could think of me was as a Viking, but those days were long gone. And they would never be back.

In hindsight, I can see that it was just too painful for most people to talk about what I had become. They figured I felt the same way, but I was more ready to face the realities of my life than people realized. Maybe I was even more ready to face real life than most of them were.

I made up my mind that if I couldn't use my legs, then I was going to be the best wheeler around. I was determined not to let my legs' destruction destroy me. There'd be no grass left growing under my wheels!

I kept busy with the Left Guard, public appearances, speaking engagements, and announcing Vikings basketball games. The drinking and partying didn't stop.

It was Susan who kept me from falling over the edge. She had wanted to get into psychiatric nursing when she graduated from the College of St. Benedict nursing program, but at the time there had been no psych positions available. She took a position instead in the rehabilitation unit at the University of Minnesota hospital. She accepted the job with the understanding that she could have the next available position in the psychiatric department. By the time that position was available, she'd become so attached to us guys in the ward that she stayed there with us.

Besides, she'd developed a *special* attachment!

SUE (SCIPIONI) KASSULKE:

I fell in love with Karl the minute I laid eyes on him. Really! It was love at first sight.

I took one look at him and said to myself, *Some day I'm going to marry that guy.* Then I thought, *How dumb, Sue. You don't even know him, and you're ready to get married!*

I'd never seen him before in my life. In fact, I didn't really know anything about him, other than that he played football. I was never that interested in football. My dad and brothers were, and they'd watch it every Sunday afternoon. But Mom and I would get disgusted and leave the room.

I knew Karl played for the Vikings, but like I told him

later, "It's not like you're Tarkenton or Lurtsema, or somebody that's famous."

He'd just laugh that crazy cackle of his.

I know that to a lot of people Karl was really a famous person, but he wasn't the quarterback, and that's who I watched on the field. And then, Lurtsema was starting to do his commercials on television, and I thought he was a stitch.

I think Karl knew that I cared about him, but then, everybody did. And I don't think he had any romantic feelings toward me at the start. But for me it was love at first sight.

Because of the problems I had with the house in Burnsville, Paul Mergens helped me find a house more suitable for me to use while living in a wheelchair. We found one in suburban Eagan and installed an elevator chair on the steps so I could also have access to the basement. From that point on I began emerging into independence.

My sister, Carmen, was still living with me. She was extremely helpful during that difficult time, and I became very dependent on her. She took care of just about every need I had with skill and kindness.

Finally Sue began to insist that I needed to learn to do things for myself. It all began to come to a head when I started taking driving lessons.

Paul had leased a van for me. We called it "Ironsides" because it was similar to the one Raymond Burr used on the television show. It had a hydraulic platform to lift my chair in and out of the van, and we travelled all over the Midwest in it. I was still involved in bars and was making many public appearances, speaking at and hosting meetings in five states.

Then Sue insisted that I learn to drive for myself. "Karl, they have hand controls now that they can put on any car. Paraplegics all over the country are using them. You should try, too."

I was thrilled at the possibility, but Carmen was afraid that it would be too much for me. "Karl, you can't take this rehabilitation thing too far."

"I suppose, sis, but I'd really like to try."

She was afraid for me. She was afraid that I would become confused, something I still did on occasion. But Sue insisted that it would be good for me to get lost while driving. I would have to figure out where I was and get home on my own.

I wanted to learn. And when the day that I received my license came, nobody was prouder of me than Carmen was. That's a sister for you!

I can understand how people without handicaps often become uncomfortable when they think of the handicapped being able to do things they have never seen them do. I used to react much the same way, but I've been convinced that the only real difference between me and someone who has full use of his legs is that I move a little slower. Sometimes.

I knew I was on my way back to independent living when I received my first speeding ticket.

The patrolman who had given me the driving test had asked me for my autograph, so I knew that I would pass that test! The one who ticketed me for speeding wasn't so understanding. He lectured me on how foolish I was to drive carelessly. He was very concerned.

"Karl, of all people you should know better than to drive like that!"

I knew he was right, but still, I was elated. I realized that I really was like everybody else, and I had a speeding ticket to prove it! I called up several of my friends to tell them about it. Hack told me that I sounded as excited as the day I was elected all-pro.

"Yeah, Hack, but I didn't get a chance to vote for myself this time!"

CHAPTER 33

The Ides of March

●

Sue and I were married in March of 1975.

We had been talking about it since October. "I don't know if I can provide for you, Sue."

I was feeling pretty low. I kept thinking of how my life had "gone to hell," and I couldn't see how I could ever support a wife. I certainly didn't want Sue to have to support me.

Sue believed that I needed encouragement. She kept forcing me to talk about it. "Karl, I think we should get married."

I couldn't see how we could get married immediately. Maybe someday. But I had no idea how I could ever support her. And besides, I was still so confused and lost. My mind wouldn't stay with a subject very long, and I often had trouble in conversation.

We finally made our decision in February, and before long our plans were on the way with a vengeance. Sue wanted to get married on my birthday, the twentieth, but March 20 was a weekday. We finally settled on Saturday the fifteenth.

"Beware the Ides of March."

We invited our immediate families and a few of our close friends. It was a simple ceremony at the house. Because I had been divorced, we couldn't be married in Sue's church. Sue did discuss the wedding with her priest, Father Bob Loftus, who attended and participated in the wedding. Rev. Glen Thorp, pastor of Bethany Presbyterian Church near the university, performed the actual ceremony.

Afterwards, we had a small reception for the wedding party at Mancini's restaurant in St. Paul. Both CBS and ABC broadcast our story on the national news that night, and friends from across the nation called to tell us they saw it. It was an exciting and glorious day!

195

A month later, Joe Duffy threw a big party for us at Duffs in the Park. It, too, was a beautiful reception, with several hundred people in attendance.

We spent our "honeymoon" at home. As a matter of fact, we weren't even alone on our wedding night.

My parents had come up from Milwaukee and were staying at our house that night. They slept in the guest bedroom. The only problem is that the guest bedroom is a little room just off the master bedroom, more like a nursery. It left us with no privacy.

We had just gotten into bed when Susan started to giggle.

"What's so funny?"

"Oh, I was just thinking about the situation. Here we are on our wedding night, and we have chaperones."

"Oh, no. I hadn't even thought about that."

"Well, what should we do?"

"Whatever, it better not be too risqué!"

Shortly after my release from the rehab center, I had begun announcing for the Vikings basketball team. I overwhelmed the audiences with my effervescent baloney! I really enjoyed announcing the games and entertaining the crowds. I still do. But because of that commitment, and my work at the Left Guard, neither Sue nor I could take off more than the weekend. I was glad for the work, but it didn't leave much time for a honeymoon. Since I didn't leave the Left Guard until that spring, our schedule stayed hectic for a long time.

Denny Weber, John Hansen, and I had started "Karl Kassulke's Viking Report" in the fall of '74. I wrote my weekly report on the Vikings' games, "astounding them with the brilliance of my observations," as I called it. It was a delightful way of keeping in touch with my friends and with the inside story of what was happening on the team. The report enjoyed some success, but with all the financial problems I faced because of the bars it soon became more than I could handle by myself. Eventually Bob Lurtsema took it over.

Also for several years I wrote a column for several newspapers in Minnesota and western Wisconsin.

Each year I have to check into the university hospital for a three-day series of studies on my renal functions. Kidney failure is one of the most frequent causes of death among both paraplegics and quadriplegics. My specialist, Dr. Mary Price, keeps very close tabs on me. She's also a delightful person, always encouraging me.

"Well, Mary, I'm here for my annual tune-up. Just check the points and plugs and give me a grease job and an oil change."

It's the same every year. Range of motion tests. Some strength tests. Renal tests. There are machines for each of them. And Mary usually has a couple of residents with her when she conducts them.

During one of my checkups Dale Hackbart came back to the university to have the vertebrae in his neck repaired. He had had his neck broken by Boobie Clark of the Cincinnati Bengels when Boobie had smashed him in the back of his head with a forearm following a play. This had happened in 1973, not long after my injury. By 1977 it was giving him enough pain that he needed surgery.

When he finally awoke after surgery, I was in his room waiting with Bev, his wife. I wheeled up real close to him, took his arm, and in my most comforting and serious tone of voice asked him, "Do you have any paralysis at all? Is there anything wrong with you? Maybe like me?"

He began to laugh.

"No, you clown. I think everything is all right."

"Good!"

I pulled out my cribbage board, and for the next three days Hackbart and I played cribbage and told stories. It was like the old days again, though it often became a three-ring circus as we tried to figure out how we would pick up the cards when they fell on the floor. To this day Sue claims that I could be on my death bed and still be trying to figure out a way of getting in one more game of cribbage.

Every night the nurses would have to kick me out of his room. They said my laugh was too loud, and the patients couldn't sleep.

Our first three years together, Sue and I lived essentially an extension of the partying, hectic existence I had lived as a Viking. We stayed out late, went to nearly every public event and grand opening, and kept a very active social schedule. We also tried to keep in touch with Kurt and Kory, as much as we were allowed to, and it was something trying to keep up with them!

We kept very busy. And there was no grass growing under my wheels. Then I began to notice a change in Sue.

She didn't seem to be as happy as she had been, and often when we would come home from some big event, she'd appear depressed and discouraged. One night I asked her what the problem was.

"Oh, I don't know. It's just that my life seems so hollow and insignificant. Something's missing, and I don't know what it is for sure."

I became very defensive. I was feeling the same way inside, but had been filling my days with activity and thus had managed to avoid thinking about it. I'd been through this once already, and I knew I couldn't handle Sue deciding to bail out on me, too.

"What do you mean, Sue?"

"Well, Karl. We've got all the friends anybody could ever want. And we seem to have a lot of good times, and money's no problem. And . . . Oh, Karl, it's not us. I love you more every day!"

"Well, at least it isn't serious, then."

"But I think it is, Karl. I think we should go talk with a priest."

"A priest? What the hell for?"

"Karl, we've been happy together from the start. We both

know that. But there's something missing, and the only thing I can imagine it could be is the church."

"The church? C'mon, Sue. I went through all that when I was a kid. Besides, we go sometimes. And I don't see anything that important about it."

"But Karl, that's just the point. We can't take communion because of your divorce, and we can't really be a part of it. I was talking with a priest the other day and he said that if you could somehow get an annulment of your first marriage, then we could get married in the church and take communion. Maybe if we could get right with the church, we could be right with God. Then everything would be alright."

I didn't know what to say. I had felt some vague uneasiness for a long time. For years. My reaction had been to cover it up with a lot of noise and laughter. But who knows?

Maybe we should talk to the priest. It couldn't hurt anything.

CHAPTER 34

A New Kind of Confession
●

It looked too easy to be true.

All we needed was five people who had been close to my previous marriage to write letters to the Tribunal of the Archdiocese of St. Paul. They were to answer a series of questions the Tribunal asked. The basic thrust was whether or not, in the opinion of the person writing the letter, both parties had ever intended to stay together for life. In short, was there a real marriage? Then the Tribunal would make a definitive judgment.

I was skeptical. "Sue, for Pete's sake! Jan and I were married eight years. They will never buy this idea at all."

"I don't know, Karl. But I do know that something's wrong between us and God. And maybe this is the only way to make it right."

All five letters were sent out and everybody returned theirs right away.

Everybody but John Campbell.

So I called John on the phone. "John, when are you going to get that letter written for us?"

"Well, Karl. I've got to think about it some more. I'm not sure what I should say."

"Well, buddy, get with it. I'm counting on you. This whole thing is really bothering Sue, and I'd like to get it over with as soon as possible."

This same conversation continued on and off—for several months. Finally one day I ran into John at the Camp Confidence Golf Tournament.

"John, I don't understand this. You're a good friend of mine, and I expected that you'd be the first one to get your letter written."

"Yeah, Karl. I guess I've been stalling you."

"John, you've got to help me on this. Sue is on pins and needles, and the priest is after me to get someone else to write that letter. But I want you to do it. You knew Jan and me. If we can just get your letter in, we can get them to make a judgment, and I'll be off the hook."

"I'll tell you what. I'll be over Monday night."

He never made it. When I saw him a few days later, he was full of apologies. "I'm sorry, Karl. I know I was wrong not to come, but I had this class at our church Monday night and just didn't know what to say."

"Yea. Well . . . OK. But c'mon. You've got to help me out on this."

This went on for another two months, and finally one day he called to let us know he'd be over that night.

When John climbed out of his car that evening, Sue began to laugh. "Karl, this must be some kind of joke. I think John is carrying a Bible with him."

"A Bible? No kidding!"

I began to laugh. John Campbell carrying a Bible. That made as much sense as Captain Kangaroo passing out *Playboy* magazines on his show.

I wheeled out to the door to greet him.

"Hiya, John. Thanks for coming."

"Hi, Karl."

Well, this wouldn't be so bad. He still had that old twinkle in his eye.

We went downstairs to the den.

"Can I get you anything, John. A beer?"

"That's OK, Karl. I don't think I want any."

Sue and I looked at each other. This was new. John could chug more beer than I did, and he was turning down a free one! He'd never done that before.

We got around the game table. John began. "I think we should pray before we start this." Sue and I both shrugged our shoulders. John prayed.

I'm not sure exactly what he said, but in essence it had

something to do with God guiding our minds and showing us what was the right thing to do.

I was thinking that maybe he'd had his bell rung one too many times. Finally he finished and turned to Sue. "Sue, why is this so important to you?"

"Well, John, it's really been bothering me that we can't be a part of the church. You know what I mean. The church says we're not really married because of Karl's first marriage. But if we can get it annulled, then we can get married in the church. And then we can both receive the sacraments and the blessings of the church. I think we'll be happy."

I could tell that this was going to get heavy, so I tried to lighten up the conversation. "C'mon, John, don't be so serious. It's only a letter. Look. I'm thirsty. How about a beer?"

John and Sue were already deep in conversation.

"Sue, do you know Jesus Christ?"

"Well . . . I guess so. I mean, I went to church and was confirmed and all that when I was a kid. And I go pretty often. So, yeah. I guess I do."

"That's not what I'm talking about, Sue. What I want to know is whether or not you've invited him into your life. Whether you've said, 'Here, Jesus. I give myself to you. Use me in this world any way you can.'"

"John, you know when you put it that way the answer has to be no."

"What about you, Karl?"

"C'mon, John, what's the big deal? I didn't ask you over here for a sermon. I asked you to write a letter for me."

"I'm coming to that, Karl. What I'm trying to say to both of you is that unless you know Jesus Christ as your Savior, and unless you make him first in your life, then it doesn't make any difference what you do about that annulment."

Sue looked very uneasy. "Do you really mean that, John?"

"You bet I do, Sue. That annulment wouldn't be worth the paper it was written on if you were to die tonight without knowing Jesus. That's why I came over here tonight. To ask you to invite him into your life."

I hit the roof.

"Damn it, John. I asked you six months ago to do this as a favor to help us out . . . to do a favor for a friend. Are you going to write that letter or not? If not, then get out of here and stop bothering Sue with all this religious talk. Besides, both of us have gone to church all our lives, and we don't get that much out of it. So what's the big deal?"

Now it was John's turn to get tough. Hehad been capable of knocking me flat on my back on the football field, and there would be no intimidating him with my shouting.

"Karl, I could have written a lot of things and sent them in for you, but my friendship with you means enough to me that I'm going to tell you why I can't do this. Face to face. If I'm willing to put our friendship on the line, I expect you to listen in return."

"OK, John. I'll listen."

"Well, in the first place, the Bible says absolutely nothing about any annulments. It does talk about divorce. But there isn't a word in this whole Bible about annulment."

"Are you sure about that, John?"

"You bet I'm sure! I've been studying this ever since you asked me to write that letter. Here, let me read something to you. Matthew 19:8: ' "Because of your stubbornness Moses let you divorce your wives," ' and just before that it says this about husbands and wives. ' "Thus they are no longer two but one flesh. Therefore, let no man separate what God has joined." ' "

I had nothing to say. I'd heard those verses at weddings, but it had never occurred to me that anybody would ever talk about them while they were discussing something important.

Sue began to question John. "So what does it mean?"

"Sue, it means that I can't do anything to pass judgment on the marriage that Jan and Karl had. And it also means that nobody else can, either. Not preachers or priests or tribunals."

He went on.

"Karl and Sue. That first marriage is over. It was sinful for it to end, but it did, and God will forgive both Jan and Karl if they ask forgiveness for it. But that marriage isn't what's important. The important thing is that you know that Jesus Christ lives in you and that you live in him. And that you'll go on living with him in heaven when you die."

"I don't think I understand what you mean."

He turned in his Bible to St. John's gospel, chapter three, and began reading about a Jewish leader named Nicodemus. He read how this Nicodemus came to Jesus at night and wanted to know what he needed to do to start his life over. Then John read where Jesus said that you must be born again and " 'No one can enter into God's kingdom without being begotten of water and Spirit.' "

Then he came to verse sixteen.

"Listen carefully, now. It says, ' "Yes, God so loved the world that he gave his only Son, that whoever believes in him may not die but may have eternal life. God did not send his Son into the world to condemn the world, but that the world might be saved through him." '

"Karl . . . Sue . . . We can put your names right in there. God so loved Karl and Sue that he gave his only Son, that if Karl and Sue believe in him they will not die but will have eternal life. That's why I couldn't write that letter for you. I'm no judge on that marriage. Only God is. But if I wrote that letter and you went on the way you are, you could so easily think that everything was fixed up between you and God. And it really isn't, is it?"

There were tears coming down Sue's face now. She was slowly shaking her head. I began to see what he was talking about.

"No, John, I don't think either Sue or I know God like that."

"Karl, I didn't either for so many years. And then not long

ago, my wife, Sue, became a Christian and began to talk to me just like I've been talking with you. I didn't like what she was saying. I got mad. Just like you, Karl. I didn't want to listen to her, and so I'd just storm out of the house. I figured I had enough problems. But finally, after watching the peace she and her Christian friends had in the face of all the troubles we were having, I gave my life to Jesus Christ, too. I've never regretted it. And I don't think I ever will."

"But how do we get things fixed up with God, John?" It was Sue speaking.

"It's so simple. The Bible says, 'whosoever therefore shall confess me before men, him I will confess also before my father which is in heaven.' That sounds like a beautiful introduction to Almighty God to me. And it happens when we ask Jesus to come into our lives."

"I think I'd like to do that, John."

"What about you, Karl?"

"Yeah. I guess so. Maybe this is what I've been looking for for so long."

"No maybes about it, Karl. I know you too well."

"Let's pray then. Karl, you go first."

I was scared to death. Suppose I started laughing and said something stupid, which I have a tendency to do. But I prayed anyway.

"Jesus, I want you to come into my life like you have for my friend, John Campbell. I want to live for you. I admit I don't know much about what that means yet, but I do want to do it. And, thanks for sending John over here tonight to talk with us."

Next it was Sue. Her prayer was so simple.

"Jesus, I don't know you either, but I want to. So please come into my heart and make me like you. Amen."

John finished with his own prayer. When he was finished, each of us had tears of joy.

The Good Shepherd had just found two more of His lost sheep.

CHAPTER 35

What's in a Name?

●

It was as if my life had suddenly started over.

In the past Sue and I would wake up in the morning, and before long we would be talking about Jan with bitterness and anger. I'd been terribly hurt by her leaving me, and I was angered by the hassles she gave me when I tried to spend time with Kurt and Kory. As a result, I carried a big chip on my shoulder. I couldn't even think about Jan without a knot forming in my stomach and bitterness rolling over me in waves.

This morning was already different. When I awakened, Sue was lying beside me with her head on her arm. She was smiling at me. "Good morning, Sweetheart! I love you."

"Aaahhh! It's that Kassulke charm at work again!"

"What are you thinking about, Karl!"

"Last night."

"Me, too."

"What do you think?"

"I feel different, like a whole burden has been lifted off my shoulders. I feel free."

"I feel the same way, too."

"And I never slept better in all my life!"

"That's a joy, to hear you say that. But I've got something else going on in my mind, too."

"What's that?"

"Jan."

"Oh, Karl. Not that again!"

"No, it's different. I just realized that the reason we've been having so much trouble with her is that none of us knew the Lord. Wouldn't it be wonderful if some day she'd come to know him, too."

Sue just stared at me.

"What's the matter?"

"What's the matter? Nothing's the matter! It's just that I've hoped so long for the day when we could talk about Jan without getting upset. And here we are, wanting for her to come to know the Lord, too. Wouldn't it be great if she would?"

We both began to laugh. This certainly was a new way to live.

Before leaving, John had told us that we should seek a manifestation in our lives to show that our prayers were answered. He said it would strengthen our conviction that Christ really was living in us. I began to wonder if this could be that manifestation.

And then the phone rang. It was John. While Sue and he talked, I held my ear close to the phone.

"How are you two feeling this morning?"

"Oh, wow!"

"A little better?"

"I've never slept better in my life."

"A new mattress could do that for you. Have you got anything better going?"

Sue told him about our concern for Jan and the boys.

"That's it, Sue. That's the manifestation you prayed for. Only Jesus Christ could change your feelings toward her like that."

It was time for John to leave for work, and so we prayed a short prayer of thanksgiving together. We were just beginning the most exciting adventure of our lives.

At first it was painful to look back and see how lost I had been. I'd grown up in a home where I was taught about God, and I had even gone through the confirmation program. At the time I took it very seriously and had been very active in the youth department in our church. But when I went off to college, I just left it behind me. My God was football, and I worshipped at its altar with enthusiasm.

All the glamor of being a hero and my preoccupation with

being the life of every party had gradually taken over. Though I had had plenty of excitement, it had turned on me and had become routine and empty.

How life came alive for me now!

In fact, it's hard to find words that can express what happened. First, we decided that we needed to go to church more regularly. We felt very awkward at our old church. The annulment came up whenever we went, and finally we decided that we probably should begin to look for another place of worship.

"After all," she said. "The annulment doesn't mean anything to us now, anyway. We know that in God's sight we're forgiven for our past, and we don't need any more hassle about it." So we began looking.

I had never realized the number of good churches in the Twin Cities. To be honest, I really hadn't paid any attention during services before, but now it seemed as if we were hearing the real meaning of words that had only been words before.

It was Sue who first talked about finding a church home. "We've been going to a different church almost every week. We really should be picking one instead of going to so many."

I felt that we would know the right one when we found it.

One evening Glen Thorp, the minister who had married us, called from Los Angeles, where he now pastors. He had heard about our commitment to Christ, and he wanted to hear it for himself. We got on both extensions and told him about the whole evening with John Campbell. We knew he and his wife, Jeanne, had been praying for us for a long time, and they were delighted to hear the good news!

Soon after we found a church we both really loved.

Another stepping stone on our new-found path was the Bible study group we joined. John and Sue Campbell introduced us to these people, people from the south side of the Twin Cities. This group has been a source of real spiritual strength and growth.

We also became reacquainted with Dick and Patti Stigman, who had led John and Sue Campbell to the Lord. Since then Dick and Patti and their family have been a real blessing to us. They have nine children, four of whom they have adopted; and like John and Sue, whenever we've needed them, Dick and Patti have been there and prayed for us. And we've needed lots of prayers!

One of the other groups we attended was a Bible study group started among the Vikings. Ron Davis, teaching pastor at Hope Presbyterian Church, did most of the teaching when we first began attending, but now John Warder, who serves as a chaplain for professional athletes in the Twin Cities, leads the group.

It's a joy to see the Vikings get together to study the Bible and pray for one another. To see these men—like Wally Hilgenberg, Jeff Siemon, Rick Danmeier, Wes Hamilton, Matt Blair, Milt Sunde, and Greg Coleman, just to name a few—together learning from the Word thrills my heart. How I rejoice when I see that nucleus of present and past players changing the lives of so many people.

I know some of the guys on the team think we've all gone off the deep end. They don't understand us, and some say of me, "Kassulke's got religion."

I *had* religion, and it did nothing for me. Now I have Jesus Christ, and there isn't an hour that goes by that I don't thank Him for what my life has become.

The real shocker, though, came when Sue came home from the doctor's office one afternoon and announced, "Guess what, Karl! We're going to have a baby!"

"A baby?"

I could hardly believe her. We had wanted to have a child together, but I thought that she was just teasing me, playing one of those practical jokes we enjoy so much.

"The doctor says the baby's due the fourth of July."

Now I was excited. I was going to be a father again! I began to yell, "AAAAHHHHH! Alright! I can't believe it! Hallelujah!"

Sue was laughing, and then I could see tears in her eyes. "Karl, don't you understand? July Fourth is exactly nine months from when we were born again. Remember how John had us ask God for a manifestation? Here's another one!"

I was shocked. I knew it could have happened like that, but this was more than a coincidence. I was overwhelmed.

Many people do not realize that paraplegia doesn't necessarily end one's sex life. Once the news got around, I couldn't believe some of the funny things that happened. Many people had assumed we had been living a life of happy celibacy for four years. Everybody was curious, but nobody seemed to want to approach the subject directly. That is until the day a man confronted me in a grocery store and asked, "What's your technique, Karl?"

I roared with laughter.

"What's yours?" I snapped.

"I guess I had that coming," was all he said.

Wally Hilgenberg's wife, Mary, was pregnant at the same time as Sue. They went through everything together—the morning sickness, the first kick. I remember one night when they were at our place Mary said that it was so different to be having a baby now that she was a Christian.

"Before, it was, 'Well, I'm pregnant.' Now, it's the excitement of creating something totally unique and new with God."

It was my turn.

"Mary, it's no different for a father. I love my two boys Kory and Kurt. I always will. But this time is special for me, too. Now it's Sue and me and God. Not just the two of us."

As it turned out, our baby was born on June 30, 1979. He didn't quite hold out for full term. We named him Christopher, which means "follower of Christ."

I pray that each of my boys will become a follower of Christ. It's the only way to live.

CHAPTER 36

Rookie Again

●

"Karl, how would you like to get into coaching?"

I must have thought about it for at least a millionth of a second before I said, "I'd love it! Man, I'd love it!"

The last of the great holdouts! My life in football had now come full circle.

It began in church, believe it or not. I had been asked to speak at Calvary Baptist Church in Roseville, Minnesota, in May of 1980. I did what I always do when I speak. I talked about my career in football and all the good things that God has done for me. I like it best when people are able to ask me their questions.

Afterwards, one man seemed particularly determined to talk with me.

"Hi, Karl. My name's George Henry."

"Nice to meet ya, George."

"It was sure good to see you, Karl. Even better to hear you talk about what God's doing in your life. I'm the athletic director at Bethel College, and I'd like to talk with you sometime, if you'd like."

I didn't know what he wanted to talk about with me, but it sounded fine. "Great! Sure. Call me anytime."

I gave him my telephone number and didn't give the incident much more thought.

A few days later he called. He wanted to come over to the house some evening with a friend of his named Dud Lutton and talk with me about an idea they both had. We set up our appointment for the next week.

By the time they arrived I was on pins and needles. The

rumor that they were going to ask me to coach had already gotten back to me, and I was so thrilled about the opportunity that I had all I could do to keep from calling George to see if they could come out to my place a couple of days early.

They were prompt, thank goodness. After the appropriate introductions we sat around together and talked for hours.

They told me about the school. Baptist. Small college. Nineteen hundred students. Strong Christian emphasis. New campus.

They told me about the staff. George was the athletic director. Dud was the head coach and new at Bethel. He had coached at Rocky Mountain College in Billings, Montana, and played at Pacific Lutheran University in Tacoma, Washington. Craig Dahl, Brad Pole, Dave Anderson, and Jon Kramka made up the rest of the coaching staff.

They talked about the program. It wasn't doing too well, but there was hope. The attitude was positive. The school administration was supportive. Scholarships were given for need, rather than just ability. They both wanted to set a strong spiritual direction for the team.

But they said nothing about a job.

Afterwards, Sue said it was like being in high school all over again, waiting for the boy your friends told you was crazy about you to get up the courage to ask for a date. Never having had that problem, I don't know about that, but I kept wondering when they were going to get on with it.

Finally they were finished with the preliminaries. And when they asked me to coach the defensive backfield, I didn't give them any time to have second thoughts before I gave them my answer.

It had been such a long road back to the game I love so much.

There had been so many detours. So many dead ends. So many disappointments. I'd always wanted to be a teacher when I finished my football career. A teacher and a coach, but I thought my injury had ended all hope of coaching.

But now I was back! And I'd be on the field soon, only this time on wheels.

I knew I'd be ready when the first whistle blew.

God had been so good to Sue and me. Most of the time we hadn't even been aware of what was going on. We were blind to His bounty, but even in the worst moments, God had been watching out for us and protecting us. Let me give you an example.

In January of 1978 I had gone into the hospital at the University of Minnesota for a surgical procedure related to my injury. Sue had brought me in around noon, and I was to have surgery the following day. We hadn't been there long when I remembered that I'd forgotten to pack my cribbage board, as well as several other personal items.

"Susan, would you mind running home and picking up my stuff? We could play some cribbage tonight."

She agreed that it was absolutely essential that I have my cribbage board at the hospital that night, so off she went, with a promise to get back by seven so we could get in a good three hours.

She called about seven o'clock. "Karl. I'm not going to be able to make it tonight. I've been in an auto accident, and I'm calling from Divine Redeemer Hospital in South St. Paul."

"Sure, Sue. And I suppose they're keeping you in the morgue, too!"

We were always playing practical jokes on one another, and I assumed that she was downstairs in the lobby.

"That's not funny, Karl. I'm serious. I was on Highway 13 going toward the Mendota Bridge at about sixty miles an hour when this lady and her car jumped right into my lane and we hit head on."

"Haw! That's a good one. C'mon, Sue, are you going to get up here with that board? I know I'm gonna whip you tonight."

"I'm serious, Karl. The car's totalled, and my face is a mess."

I still didn't believe her, but when the doctor got on the line to tell me that Sue had been in a very bad accident but that she was in good condition, I was ready to go home. Sue finally got me calmed down.

"Karl, they say I can go home tonight. My brother Mark is here with me, and Mom and Dad are going to come down from Virginia and stay with me at the house for a few days. I'll be alright. You go ahead with your surgery."

I did, and since Sue wasn't able to get up to see me, I insisted on being released after three days, rather than the week to ten days that the doctors recommended.

When I saw Sue I was sickened. I couldn't believe my eyes. Her eyes were swelled nearly shut, and her face looked like a black and blue puff ball. She was in such pain.

"Oh, Sue. How could anybody do this to you? What can I do to help?"

Then I got mad. My life had been messed up badly enough by one careless driver, and now another one had messed up Sue's beautiful face. It was a mass of stitches and bruises and lumps of every size and shape.

We had already been in one serious wreck in Winona, Minnesota, when an eighty-year-old man had run a red light and caused a wild chain-reaction accident. Our car had been totalled that time, too. Maybe the world had it in for us when we were on the road. I couldn't take the thought of losing Sue, and when I saw what had happened to her I was afraid.

"It is scary, Karl. But just think what could have happened if I hadn't been wearing that seat belt. That's what saved my life, just like in Winona." And so we told all our friends that it was because Sue was wearing that seat belt that she hadn't been killed. Fortunately, she had a complete recovery, and her face is as beautiful as it always was.

The thought that God had been protecting us in those dangerous situations had never occurred to either of us. There was no reason why it would have then, but now that we know how bad things could have been—for me in my motor-cycle accident and for Sue in hers—and especially now that we know how much God loves us and how good He is to us, we know why we weren't killed in those accidents. We were being protected. For what reason only God really knows.

It's really very difficult to communicate to others just how good God has been to me in my life and the gratitude that I feel. Most people get very uncomfortable when I talk about this, as if they have some suffering in their own lives that they're not willing to give up to the Lord, but it is true. God has been so good to me. And my recovery from the accident is a modern-day miracle, a living illustration of the grace of God at work today.

Not only was I completely baffled at the time of my accident by why the doctors couldn't just fix me up like they had with all my other injuries and send me on my merry way again, but I was completely incapable of knowing how to cope with the reality of what it would mean to spend the rest of my life in a wheelchair. I was too confused to understand, and even my confusion at that time was God's goodness to me.

I kept insisting that I'd be back on my feet and ready to play football in time for the playoffs, while the doctors' big concern was whether I'd ever be able to live in a wheelchair or whether I'd have to be institutionalized with round-the-clock care. Only the goodness of God brought me back into touch with reality and gave my independence to me again.

For a long time I had a hard time putting the ends of sentences with their beginnings. What I said sounded fine, until you bothered to listen. I literally couldn't remember what had happened a few seconds earlier. But today my memory has nearly completely returned, though there still is a blank around the time of the accident. The healing of my mind shows more of God's goodness to me.

While I was in the hospital after the motorcycle accident, I had forgotten that my marriage had ended; I never could figure out why Jan and the boys weren't visiting me. I'd talk about it with Sue and the other nurses and whenever the boys would be brought up to see me by one of Jan's friends, I'd talk about them for days, telling everybody who would listen to me how I was going to move back home with my family someday and things would get better. Today I have a lovely wife and a third son. Kurt and Kory have grown to become strong young men whom I love with all my heart. And they love me as their father. God has given me all this.

As I lay there in the hospital and listened to my teammates talk about the good old days and the championships and all the great moments we had shared, I would remember. Some of it, at least. And though I knew it was all over, I would have given anything to be able to get back on the field again. And now God has even given football back to me, too.

I wish that I could say that I helped Bethel become a small college powerhouse, that we had a great season and a winning team. It would make a perfect story.

We didn't.

But we were all winners.

We won only two games on the field, but we really won a lot more than that. We saw young men (and some women) make sound, sure commitments to Jesus Christ through what happened on that team. And we saw guys go into the locker rooms as losers and come out as winners. A group of young men who began the year as highly independent individuals ended it as a team.

That is what I think football should be.

As coaches we hoped to establish a spiritually healthy climate on the team and help the team build a real sense of teamwork. We stressed these elements during the week in practice, and following every game, win or lose, we spent over thirty minutes sharing our appreciation for one another as persons, both for good play and for working together. Prayer followed, thanking God for the joy of being able to compete and the privilege of playing football for Him.

Corny? It depends on your point of view. But I've never felt a truer sense of team spirit and commitment to one another on a team than I saw among those young men.

It wasn't easy to coach from a wheelchair. But it was a delight.

I've become used to the normal aggravations that go with living in a wheelchair. Coaching from one created some new problems, though. Being an old defensive back, I often found it frustrating not to be able to demonstrate what I wanted done. Brad Pole, another coach, did a wonderful job demonstrating the drills and basic techniques of the defensive backfield to the players, but it wasn't the same as being able to do it myself. At times my heart ached for the chance to get down there with the guys, to roll around on the ground, feeling the dirt on my fingers and smelling that special smell that grass only has when you've crashed into it after hitting a 200-pound tight end.

Actually I did manage to get down there on the ground with the guys a few times.

Bethel fixed up a specially designed and equipped motor scooter for me. Like my car, it had hand controls and I used it to get from place to place during practice. I also had a wheelchair that I used while coaching.

And yes, I fell off! More than once.

It was a little embarrassing. Being confined to a scooter and wheelchair prevented me from getting as physically close to the players as I would have liked. I'm a great believer in the coach bumping shoulders with the guys and standing toe-to-toe and eye-to-eye with them. The communication of what you want done goes beyond mere words, and I miss that part of coaching. Somehow I'll find a way to overcome that.

And besides, next season I won't be a rookie any longer!

Even in this I have known God's goodness, and I am so thankful for the opportunity to be back in football. Thankful to Dud and George for having the courage to hire me. And to the Lord.

There are times, friends, when the growin' grass under the wheels does feel good!

CHAPTER 37

A New Joy
●

Frequently someone will say, "It's too bad you were injured like that, Karl. I don't think I could handle being paralyzed."

When I was first injured, I understood that point of view better. I, too, felt it was a low blow. But time has a way of changing a man's perspective.

And Christ has changed that and a lot more.

I've now come to see that often what we think of as being bad turns out for our good. Only God really knows for sure.

Recently, a friend gave me a copy of Keith Miller's book, *A Habitation of Dragons*. With a title that vivid, I thought it deserved to be read!

When I came to the place my friend had marked for me, God showed me the meaning of my injury. Let me share it with you.

We were in a small group of adults who were struggling together to learn how to pray and to live as Christians. We were getting acquainted by going around the room, each telling the others some things about his childhood. One older lady had had a good many disappointments and seemed bitter about her past. Then it was Alice's turn. She spoke to us hesitantly.

"When I was a tiny little girl, I was put in an orphanage. I was not pretty at all, and no one wanted me. But I can recall longing to be adopted and loved by a family as far back as I can remember. I thought about it day and night. But everything I did seemed to go wrong. I tried too hard to please everybody who came to look me over, and all I did was drive people away. Then one day the head of the orphanage told me a family was going to come and take me home with them. I was so excited, I jumped up and down and cried. The matron reminded me that I was on trial and that it might not be a permanent arrangement. But I just knew it would be. So I went with this family and started to school in their town—a very happy little girl. And life began to open for me, just a little.

"But one day, a few months later, I skipped home from school and ran in the front door of the big old house we lived in. No one was at home but there in the middle of the front hall was my battered old suitcase with my little coat thrown over it. As I stood there and looked at that suitcase, it slowly dawned on me what it meant . . . they didn't want me. And I hadn't even suspected."

Alice stopped speaking a moment, but we didn't notice. We were each standing in that front hall with the high ceiling, looking at the battered suitcase and trying not to cry. Then Alice cleared her throat and said almost matter-of-factly, "That happened to me seven times before I was thirteen years old."

I looked at this tall, forty-year-old, gray-haired woman sitting across the room and wept. I had just met Alice, but I found myself loving her and feeling a great compassion for her. She looked up, surprised and touched at what had happened to us as we had responded to her story. But she held up her hand and shook her head slightly, in a gesture to stop us from feeling sorry for her. "Don't" she said with a geniunely happy smile. "I *needed* my past. You see—it brought me to God."*

Obviously, I didn't think that I needed that motorcycle accident. But that was what it took to bring me to my knees. I don't think I ever would have done it otherwise. It was what I needed.

It was God's grace to me.

And I thank Him for it.

You see, I had ten years of success.

And I didn't have anything.

When I say that I upset a lot of people. So many people

---

*From Keith Miller, *Habitation of Dragons,* copyright © 1970. Used by permission of Word Books, Publisher, Waco, Texas 76796.

strive for what I had, desperately wanting to think that success will fill their lives with joy and meaning. But success is not enough. Why pretend that it is?

I have had all the success anybody could ever want, not to mention a lot of fun. Much of it was clean. Some wasn't. But fun was all I was living for. And in the process I did hurt some people, especially my family. All those good times look pretty juvenile and hollow from today's perspective.

At the same time, I don't want to devalue my experiences as a professional football player or the people I knew then in any way. They were wonderful people, for the most part; and it is an honor to have played with the Vikings. The camaraderie of the team, the recognition from the fans, and the meaningful friendships I formed while I was a Viking are all priceless memories.

I enjoyed living most of those moments, and I enjoy remembering them today. But they weren't enough to fill the empty void in my soul. Nor would they be enough to fill the empty spot in yours, either.

They wouldn't bring you the joy I've found.

I have learned something that I wouldn't trade for all the money and fame in the world. I've learned that knowing the Lord is everything. And without the Lord, there just isn't anything solid to hang on to in this world.

I've never been happier than I have been since becoming a Christian. Sue and I always had a lot of fun, but we enjoy our lives far more today as Christians than we ever did before we knew the Lord. My life has become a celebration of joy—an air of happiness stays with us even in uncomfortable situations. I know that I can take any problem I have straight to the Lord, and he will show me the way to find the answers.

Don't let me mislead you into thinking that my life has been a bed of roses since I became a Christian. I've had my share of troubles. But every time, no matter how bad it looks, we've prayed, and there has been a way through it. The difference now is that we can have peace about our problems because we know that God truly loves us and will take care of us no matter what happens.

I believe that the most important lesson we learned was the changing of our values. Whereas we used to live primarily for a "good time," now we find ourselves staying home more and getting closer to each other. We have found that we don't need to clutter up our lives with parties every night and material objects. And that we can have just as much fun at a Bible study as we used to have at a cocktail party.

Besides, we don't wake up with a headache the next morning!

In fact, we have discovered that we can have even *more* enjoyment at the Bible study than at the cocktail party, because we talk about subjects that are important and lasting, rather than just about our new gadgets or who said what to whom. And we've found a new freedom to be honest with how we are really doing, rather than having to put up the all-sufficient front that we maintained for so long.

I've come to know and like myself better since coming to know the Lord. Other than the fact that I wheel instead of walk, I'm no different from anybody else. I enjoy my life immensely, even more than I did when I was walking. My life is filled with love and joy, and I am finally at peace with myself.

Recently, a well-meaning lady asked me why I hadn't prayed for healing.

"Karl, if you would let him, the Lord would heal you."

I would enjoy walking again someday, and someday when I get to heaven I believe I will. That isn't to make light of healing. After all, God has healed my troubled mind, as well as my heart and soul. But I had to remind this person that I don't have to have a miracle to convince myself or anybody else that I have faith.

I know that the Lord is real. I don't need to prove it to anybody.

What I really want is for my attitudes and life to show everyone how real God's love is, just as I experience it. I want them to see that God has made all the difference in my life. And I don't have to be healed for it to be real.

I look at people, and I see them trying so hard to reach for something they cannot get, or can't even define. I see them absorbed in money or success or status, and I say to myself, "Yeah, Karl, baby. You've gone through that stuff, but now you're whole. You don't need it."

So I thank God daily for Jesus Christ. Because of Him I know that when my life on earth is over, I will be with God forever. My faith is not just from reading a book, although if all I had was the Bible's promise it would be enough.

My faith grows each day because I *haven't* had to wait until I die to be with the Lord. I'm with Him every day, and He's with me.

I'm certainly not perfect, or even a "good" Christian. For openers, I feel like I've only begun to grow. I constantly feel that my walk with God is paltry, especially when I see how others love and give so much. But the truth that makes me rejoice is that I don't have to be perfect. God loves me just the way I am.

I will say this, though. I'm learning more each day what it means to live unto the Lord.

I'm wheeling for Jesus, now.

And I'd like to invite you to do so, too!

There'll be no grass growing under these wheels.
I've got a whole new life to live.